It's in Their DNA: What and Why Men and Women Do Not Ask And Do Not Answer

It's in Their DNA:

What and Why

Men and Women

Do Not Ask

And

Do Not Answer

Owen Watson, Ph.D.

TURN THE PAGE
IN YOUR LIFE

It's in Their DNA: What and Why Men and Women Do Not Ask
and Do Not Answer

Author Owen Watson's books may be purchased for educational,
business, or sales promotional use. For information, please email:
drowenwatson@outlook.com or visit www.drowenwatson.com

First Edition

Cover Design By: Owen Watson, Ph.D.

Editor: Ramona L. Watson, Ph.D.

Library of Congress Cataloging-in-Publication Data

ISBN-978-1-957420-04-2

Dedication

This project is dedicated to those who are either pursuing or in a relationship. The writing and inspiration for this book is birthed from relationship conversations with a group of singles and couples from various backgrounds, with over 585 years of experiences living life. Each person contributed "I wish I had known…" questions (that are rarely asked while dating and/or married) toward this project for the nurturing of other singles and married couples. Being a good judge of character begins by having decent and mature conversations. It is better to utilize wisdom now rather than losing valuable time later engaging in avoidable damaging experiences.

Contents

Questions From Women That Men Do Not Answer

In Closing

Note

Acknowledgements

A heartfelt thanks to each of the following persons for providing some of the most intriguing questions:

Donna Hardaway-Adams
Jamie Hornsby
Beverly Jones
Johnnie Kee
Natasha King
George Lassiter
Stacie Madkins
Kenneth McPherson
Adrienne Mims
Jonathan Rosario
Frederic Sanon
Calvin Williams, Jr.

Introduction

When it comes to encountering hurdles while dating and/or during marriage, most, if not all of us, at some points have either said, thought, or acted out an attitude of "this is not what I signed up for!" Unfortunately, truth be told, we thoughtlessly did "sign-up" for who we partnered with and what is happening or being discovered about them – whether good or bad. You see, as human beings our natural instincts drive many of us to be easily sold on selfish and misguided perceptions and wishful thinking rather than careful and thorough inspections.

Far too long have we been wrapped in the hopes of what and how we visualize a mate to be based on their looks and witnessing their best performances while dating. In doing so, we fail to take the time to ask meaningful questions and dissect indispensable information that comes from courting conversations along with subtle cautions that we see (and naively dismiss). Hence, why I've decided to switch things up a bit with this latest release by providing slightly humorous enlightenment through analyzing relationship questions, from the viewpoints of both males and females.

Medically defined, deoxyribonucleic acid (DNA) carries genetic instructions for the development, functioning, growth and reproduction of every living species. However, for this project the acronym DNA will be used as a double entendre for learning about men and women based on examining questions that genders (D)O (N)OT (A)SK and (D)O (N)OT (A)NSWER.

During times of dating, many of us are caught up in the moment and become diffident about asking certain questions due to possibly feeling they may cause a rift in our progress in the relationship. What we fail to realize is the damage it can cause by not knowing the answers to serious questions prior to getting in over our heads. With that in mind, I've taken the liberty of soliciting family and friends to acquire a total of 150 questions that inquiring minds may want, need, and/or should know when either in a relationship or pursuing one.

Not all 150 questions are meant to be asked because not all pertain to your relationship concerns or situation. However, they all shall serve as a guide to select from for asking, answering, and understanding what is most meaningful to you personally in a relationship. The first two sections are questions that men and women do not ask but should (depending on which ones matters most in your relationship). The most plausible reasons for asking the questions are individually and plainly addressed, along with supporting biblical scripture(s). The final two sections are questions that men and women do not answer. Probable reasons for why they do not answer are individually and plainly addressed, along with biblical scripture(s).

To help better understand conversations when asking any of the questions, I've constructed and am providing three factors to be used for examining your (potential) partner's responses. Those three factors are content, attitude, and transparency or C.A.T for short:

1. **Content**: substance of the answer, whether it be in his/her attitude or the very words he/she provides as an answer.
2. **Attitude** – whether it is nonchalant, offended, or defensive
   a. Nonchalant [relaxed] – signifies he/she is open for further discussion and possible change.

b. Offended [loss of words] – signifies being insulted and/or put on the stand for being judged; may be considered a slight misunderstanding on his/her part, which will require reassurance from you not only with this question but any question.

c. Defensive [self-justifying; evasive] – signifies he/she is a stickler for continuing the same path out of habit/learned behavior (strongly believes there's nothing faulty about his/her habit/learned behavior); may be a challenge to come to an agreeable compromise that would benefit you both in the future.

3. **Transparency** – whether fluid (he/she is responding off-the-cuff with an answer to please you – potential mate/life partner), or sincere (truthful).

When employing C.A.T., for the most part it should either line up with your intuition about a person, and/or at least help decipher their true character. The one thing you don't want to do is be indiscreet and creepy. Wisely utilize the times together while dating and ask questions sparingly. It is strongly recommended that C.A.T. be discreetly utilized throughout the dating phase to enhance the knowledge of your husband/wife to be for the sake of bettering expectations in the relationship.

Questions Men Do Not Ask Women but Should

Questions
Men Do Not Ask Women
but Should

1. How does your upbringing shape your attitude about money?

Some say, "I believe in spending it as it comes becomes no one is promised tomorrow."
Some say, "I believe in saving every penny and only spending on what is needed."
Some say, "We never talked about money in our home."
Some say, "We never had money to talk about in our home."

When a man asks this question to a woman, he's truly interested in knowing her financial intelligence as he simultaneously and inconspicuously gages how it may or may not complement or enhance his learned perspectives about money. Unfortunately, there are many men suffering financially while dating or in their marriages because of their significant others' attitudes and beliefs about money being contrary to theirs. Sadly, the suffering comes after investing much love and time in the individual, making it difficult to either cut ties (if dating) or have an amiable conversation about money (if married). Imagine having to constantly deal with working extra jobs, 70+ hour work weeks, working many years beyond planned retirement just to make ends meet, and paying bills that are piling up and/or not being paid due to frivolous spending habits. This is a definite stressor and a quick way to end a relationship and kill a man's zeal for working toward a (previously attainable) goal.

For most men, the pinnacle of success is summed up in having financial freedom. Wherefore, to not have financial freedom is to have an overwhelming, and at times, unbearable burden which triggers his emotions (mood swings). Such a situation is sure to create a paradox between his first thoughts and envisioned life with the woman and the reality of how he pictures her now [i.e., as the burden]. Mature men seek women with whom they can intelligently plan and build for the benefit of both. The result of "empty pockets" love is a condemned home.

Proverbs 14:1 (NIV): *The wise woman builds her house, but with her own hands the foolish one tears hers down.*

NOTE: Bear in mind C.A.T.

2. What are your spending priorities?

MEN to WOMEN: "You'd like to have your nails and hair taken care of? No problem, I'll make that happen for you. You need assistance with childcare or a bill? No worries, I got you. You need spending money to hang with your girls. Here you go, I take care of mine." All the while, he's frustrated with himself for giving what he really didn't have to give, putting himself in a bind with his legal responsibilities [i.e., personal bills].

All too often during the courting/whooing and dating stage of a normal relationship, men find themselves catering to the spending priorities of a woman in the name of supposed "love." This is a terrible precedence to set in a relationship. Without a doubt and rightfully so she will expect what he is doing now to continue throughout the relationship, possibly into marriage. This is really no fault of hers, she's simply responding to what she perceptually knows as "truth" about him – that he can afford to do what he's doing.

Justly by nature, men are wired for ensuring their spouse's every need is taken care of. However, this is not so during the dating phase, which is where many men fail the test. The young lady you're dating is not your spouse (yet) so never start what you can't maintain! When men throw out financial bait to women, they frequently find themselves being preyed upon and broke. Being out of order with your spending will always keep holes in your pockets.

When a man asks about a woman's spending priorities, he's looking for that potential mate who not only respects financial responsibilities but also who is self-disciplined and not overly materialistic. Discussing spending priorities is very important for both parties who are seriously seeking a married life together and it warrants discussion prior to marriage.

For believers, the priority of spending should begin by both of you spending time with God in prayer and in His word. From there, the priority of spending your financial resources should be dedicating an established percentage to your place of worship followed by however you both agree and deem as most significant to least in the building of your financial security as one.

3

Proverbs 3:9-10 (AMP): *Honor the LORD with your wealth and with the first fruits of all your crops (income); then your barns will be abundantly filled and your vats will overflow with new wine.*

NOTE: Bear in mind C.A.T.

3. When do you plan to retire and how will you afford it?

"I'm living for today because no one is promised tomorrow."
"I'm working on being my own boss and owning my own business."

Those are just a couple of answers a man can expect when asking a woman, "When do you plan to retire and how will you afford it?" While there is nothing wrong with neither of the answers, they do little for providing a peace of mind for the man. A guy that's asking a woman this question is a guy who is focused and sincerely seeking a partner who's willing to put in equal efforts and passions toward a financially secured future. The future can only look bright when one digs through the dirt [i.e., puts in the work] toward the light.

Proverbs 6:6-8 (NLT): *Take a lesson from the ants, you lazybones. Learn from their ways and become wise! Though they have no prince or governor or ruler to make them work, they labor hard all summer, gathering food for the winter.*

NOTE: Bear in mind C.A.T.

4. How many jobs have you had?

Old adage: "She goes through men like she goes through jobs."

And, you ask why this is an important question for men to ask women? The answer is to eliminate wasting time with someone who's considered unstable, uncommitted, and misguided. Though there are overwhelmingly positive and legitimate reasons for a woman to have had multiple jobs, it is the reason of doing so "just because" that doesn't sit well in the mind of a man. That response triggers the notion of an impatient woman: living for the upkeep of a pretentious comfortable life that satisfies the moment; seeking a temporary "sugar daddy"; and/or being immature about life, career and relationships. It suggests her thought process and practices regarding success and relationships are marred by selfishness. This is not a submittal that she's a "bad" person, but it is a warning that she's not mate ready.

Proverbs 23:4 (NIV): *Do not wear yourself out to get rich; do not trust your own cleverness.*

NOTE: Bear in mind C.A.T.

5. What's your idea of a man?

"He needs to cater to me, take care of the bills, and recognize I'm my own!"
"All he has to do is be with me, I'll take care of the rest."

Yes, both answers are extreme, however they are negatively gaining traction as examples of women's ideas of what a man is.

These type answers can be counted as statements derived from environment and/or selfishness. Nonetheless, the answer to this question can help a man either invest forward in the relationship or save a lot of time, effort, and possible heartache by severing the relationship (or the possibility of it).

Once a woman states what her idea of a man is, the ball is in the man's court for examining whether his character, resources, and ambition correspond. Although it is important for a man to recognize and realize that it's okay to not measure up to her idea of a man, it is more important that he not under- or oversell being a man. A woman's idea is not meant to define the absolute man, it's just what she's seeking a man to be in her life. He either fits the mold, decides whether he's willing and able to make the necessary adjustments, or sees it as a relationship that's not worth the investment.

For most men, finding that special woman worth the investment of life together means they both can visualize a mutual exchange of love, partnership, and high regard for one another. What no man should do is falsely fit into a woman's idea of a man out of infatuation. Doing so only sets himself up for hearing those words that any man would dread to hear from a woman, "I thought you were a real man!"

Ephesians 5:28-29 (NCV): *In the same way, husbands should love their wives as they love their own bodies. The man who loves his wife loves himself. No one ever hates his own body, but feeds and takes care of it. And that is what Christ does for the church.*

NOTE: Bear in mind C.A.T.

6. How many intimate partners have you had?

"Why do you need to know that?"

That response alone is reason enough to run! Seriously speaking, in most instances the answer to this question initiates an onslaught of follow-on questions regardless of the number of partners – consider yourself warned! So, why would a man ask a woman this question? Many men would consider this a need-to-know question (as well as follow-on questions): to evaluate whether or not it's a relationship worth the risk of having to possibly deal with past interferences [i.e., drama]; for the sake of integrity of his image; and weighing whether he's enough to meet her needs. By nature, men do not like drama, a man wants a woman who complements his image, and a man wants to be secure in knowing he's the complete answer in fulfilling intimate relations with his wife. No man should relinquish his life's peace for a temporary "piece". It is beneficial for every man to exercise wisdom and caution toward the woman of his choosing for life.

Proverbs 11:22 (NLT): *A beautiful woman who lacks discretion is like a gold ring in a pig's snout.*

NOTE: Bear in mind C.A.T.

7. How many relationships have you been in?

"Only a few, around 12."

Not an answer a man would like to hear but needs to know. Upon hearing the answer, he is now questioning her on the spot in his mind, "Why so many relationships?" Men who are seriously looking for a lifetime spouse are not impressed nor drawn by a woman with a record of many relationships. For a man, a woman having numerous past relationships is a sign of her being unstable (physically and emotionally), easy (sexually), and/or mentally touched – in other words, a trigger of caution has been released. In most cases, although the men of her past may have been the problem and not her, neither of the signs the current man is thinking of appeal nor scream marriage material to him. Furthermore, depending on her age, it will be a difficult road for a man to attempt to measure up to (or exceed) the highest points of experiences she's had with other men.

Proverbs 7:25-27 (NLT): *Don't let your hearts stray away toward her. Don't wander down her wayward path. For she has been the ruin of many: many men have been her victims. Her house is the road to the grave. Her bedroom is the den of death.*

NOTE: Bear in mind C.A.T.

8. Do you still have any feelings for your ex?

"I may think about him sometime, but it doesn't mean much because it only makes me a little upset."

Depending on the answer to this question, it can either signify danger ahead, proceed with caution, or go all in. It would be danger ahead if her answer is "yes" or vague [i.e., like "it's complicated"] – that means there's a bit of a fire still burning within her that hasn't been extinguished. For a man to proceed forward with a woman in this state would be risky, unless the man is temporarily going along, with an ulterior motive himself. On the other hand, if she is adamant and her actions are somewhat evident regarding not having feelings for her ex, a man should proceed with caution. Why with caution? Because some people, especially women, are great at hiding what they would not like for a man to know. Does this caution warrant being paranoid? Certainly not! There's a gift of intuition within each of us – use it! If you're not totally convinced that she's over her ex, trust what she's saying but verify her actions – Is there any ongoing links between them? Is she wanting to visit/hang around with his family and friends "just because"? Does she keep gifts, cards, or letters he has given her? Plainly advised, be wise without appearing creepy. Lastly, go all in if you are confidently sure (without reservation) there's no lingering connections with an ex and she meets criteria for being your spouse.

Proverbs 6:27 (NLT): *Can a man scoop a flame into his lap and not have his clothes catch on fire?*

NOTE: Bear in mind C.A.T.

9. What's the longest you've ever held a job?

"Long enough to get paid."

A relationship is more than just being in love. With all cards on the table, a man needs to know and weigh whether he's willing to be in a relationship with him being the primary bread winner and having an occasional financial contributing partner; in a relationship where they are both on the same page as contributing financial partners; or if one will take care of the home and the other bring in the finances. Often sad but true, relationships tend to have higher expectations when it comes to financial involvements rather than with love—this explains why financial issues are the leading causes of divorce. Men haphazardly go into relationships leading to marriage based on the present appeal of a woman [i.e., beauty, cleanliness, respect, etc.]. The wake-up call comes after the mountain-top high of marriage, frivolous spending, and mounting bills. He needs to know and trust that her "I Love You" translates into pulling alongside him with financial contributions toward coming up out of the valley.

Proverbs 10:4 (NLT): *Lazy people are soon poor; hard workers get rich.*

NOTE: Bear in mind C.A.T.

10. When you say you're an entrepreneur, what do you really mean?

"I have a plan, but I haven't quite put it into action."

A man looking for a relationship with an entrepreneurial-minded woman indicates the seriousness he has for a prosperous future with his spouse. By asking this question, it helps him to screen for character qualities of diligence, tenacity, and purpose. Oftentimes, having and sharing entrepreneurial aspirations complements and strengthens a relationship by way of reciprocal understanding, respect, and support for one another. It's best to observe this while dating rather than finding it out after marriage. It makes for a terrible situation when a woman shares with a man all of her high-minded ideas about her plans only for him to witness never seeing anything put into action.

Proverbs 21:5 (NIV): *The plans of the diligent lead to profit as surely as haste leads to poverty.*

NOTE: Bear in mind C.A.T.

11. Are you legally allowed on school premises?

MAN: I have to go pick my kids up from school.
WOMAN: I'll stay at the house until you return with them.
MAN: How come you never go with me to get them?
WOMAN: I don't have time for this. I'll just go back to my place for now and talk to you later.

Men, read between the lines! There are men who have either sole, primary, or joint custody of their kids and must take every necessary precaution to protect them. Unfortunately, we are living in a chaotic world where there is pedophilia, including women on the prowl. If you are a man with children, don't be afraid, over-confident, or too wrapped up in her to not ask this important question. Not only ask the question, put her to the test. If she's a person you are seriously considering to be your wife and a stepmother to your children, you have a right to know!

Luke 17:2 (NLT): *It would be better to be thrown into the sea with a millstone hung around your neck than to cause one of these little ones to fall into sin.*

NOTE: Bear in mind C.A.T.

12. Can I see your résumé?

"I've been working for a top 100 Forbes company for about 20 years."

Anyone can impress anyone with the right words. A man being in a serious relationship (soon to be married) deserves truth. Truth of knowing whether she is working and where she works. He shouldn't be made to find out later that she never held a job or is doing a job that he may consider demeaning. It's fair to say that men pride themselves in knowing their partners are truthful and functioning for the success and interest of their relationship.

James 2:18 (NLT): *Now someone may argue, "Some people have faith; others have good deeds." But I say, "How can you show me your faith if you don't have good deeds? I will show you my faith by my good deeds."*

NOTE: Bear in mind C.A.T.

13. What would your ex tell me about you?

"He'll probably say I was the one that got away."

This is a question that a man can use to build his legacy upon with a specific woman who has a high potential to be his wife. He generally listens for good and bad information and goes with whichever carries the most weight. If the negative outweighs, he takes it as a warning and the chances of entering a long-term relationship are immediately sunk. If positive outweighs, he then sets a personal challenge of making life much better with and for her. For the serious guy, the positive feedback confirms he has hit the jackpot and he begins visualizing a life of togetherness with her. That's when the door is open for her to reel him in through marriage conversations which he soon obliges with a proposal. Now if she provides negative feedback of what she believes her ex would say about her, there's a strong chance of some truth in it and it's shameful on her part.

Proverbs 12:4 (NLV): *A good wife is the pride and joy of her husband but she who brings shame is like cancer to his bones.*

NOTE: Bear in mind C.A.T.

14. Can I have a talk with your ex?

"I don't think that's a good idea."

Heed her warning, it may not be a good idea. But if she and her ex's relationship ended amicably, there should be no issue speaking with him. Here's the catch. This question is really for an evaluation of her answer, not so much for the man to act upon. Does she appear as if she is attempting to divert the man from finding out something about her and the ex or possibly damaging information about her? Or is she hesitantly saying "go for it" in hopes he doesn't? If something is observed or feels shady regarding her responsiveness, the man may want to do follow-up discreet questioning with her family or friends. If there are no negative intuitions or indications of something more, chances are she's being truthful. In all honesty, rarely does any man want to have any type of communication with his partner's ex. However, it is imperative for a man to exercise wisdom in relationship building. Know what you know without a doubt!

Proverbs 24:3 (NIV): *By wisdom a house is built, and through understanding it is established.*

NOTE: Bear in mind C.A.T.

15. What is your credit score?

"Are you serious?"

Your answer should be an emphatically resounding, "YES!" There are far too many horror stories of men getting into relationships with women who have terrible credit scores. If married, those credit scores can cost you financially when it comes time to combining finances and making joint purchases, especially buying a house. The lower the credit score, the higher the interest to be paid which will affect your quality of life in more than one way. Having and maintaining a good credit score (700-749) or a great credit score (750 and above) is ideal and shows one's character, discipline, and integrity. A credit score can be the deciding factor of living in a house, apartment, or on the street. It doesn't necessarily have to be the deal breaker for marriage, but it is worth consideration for the type of future you're planning to have. Though she may be sweet and fine as heaven, her credit score can make your life a living hell.

Proverbs 24:27 (NLT): *Do your planning and prepare your fields before building your house.*

NOTE: Bear in mind C.A.T.

16. Were you born this gender?

"Why in the world would you ask me that?"

The abominable acts rejected by God in the past have now become the accepted and protected, all-inclusive 'anything goes', godless acts of today. It would be a devastating shame for a man not to ask now and find out after marriage that his bride isn't the biological female he accepted her as being. Oh, how his heart may have long envisioned conceiving biological naturally-birthed children with his bride. During the dating phase, she may have agreed that she too would like to have children with the man but never disclosed that she couldn't naturally produce and why. The damage doesn't stop there. The everlasting effect boils over into his spirituality, if he's a man of faith and a believer of God's design of male and female. Furthermore, it exposes his manhood to open humiliation. Although it may not be politically correct and acceptable in the secular sight of this day and age, it is of the utmost significance that men of faith make it a point to always ask.

Genesis 5:2 (NIV): *He created them male and female and blessed them. And he named them "Mankind" when they were created.*

NOTE: Bear in mind C.A.T.

17. Are you legally married?

"What difference does it make?"

Men of integrity (if you don't have any, get some) think about your life being literally at stake. Don't always assume the woman you're interested in or dating (maybe hoping to marry) is single. We're living in a day and age where marriages are splitting but never lawfully dissolved. Some manage to remain in a separated state for years while both parties move on living lives as though they're single. If there are no official papers on file with the courts and that can be produced to show either a legal annulment or divorce, they are still legally married. Cut that relationship and/or hopes of one off immediately! Do not find it acceptable to be in such type of relationship, especially if you're a man of faith. Continuing in a relationship with that woman dishonors her, her husband, you, and God. If she's serious about you, she'll honor your wishes and either make things right with her husband or right by law [i.e., divorce]. However, since she's already proved to you that she has no problem being with you while legally married to her husband, what's to stop her from doing the same to you? Don't be smitten by the kitten. Men, do yourselves a solid and find out whether she's legally married. If so, deuces! Stick with God and allow Him to guide you to who He has prepared you for and her for you.

Hebrews 13:4 (NLT): *Give honor to marriage and remain faithful to one another in marriage. God will surely judge people who are immoral and those who commit adultery.*

NOTE: Bear in mind C.A.T.

18. How often do you drink?

"Occasionally."

There's responsible drinking and then there's punch bowl drunkenness. Men, know whether your partner drinks as well as how much/often she does. The subtle effects can easily and quickly become a dependency and fill a home with overwhelming sorrows. Like any central nervous system (CNS) depressant, it slows down brain functioning which creates an inability to react quickly – hence why it is against the law to drink while operating a motorized vehicle. Is drinking alcohol wrong? Certainly NOT! Can a relationship with a woman who drinks work out? DEFINTELY! Can a relationship with a woman who is a drunkard work out? HIGH RISK OF NOT! It's important to understand the consequences of being married to someone who's susceptible to becoming an addict or is an addict and weighing whether it's a risk you're prepared to take. Like the old liquor commercial says, "Don't let the good taste fool you!"

Proverbs 23:31-33 (LB): *Don't let the sparkle and the smooth taste of strong wine deceive you. For in the end it bites like a poisonous serpent; it stings like an adder. You will see hallucinations and have delirium tremens, and you will say foolish, silly things that would embarrass you to no end when sober.*

NOTE: Bear in mind C.A.T.

19. Are you greedy for me?

"Hold on, I'm not into cannibalism."

Fortunately so, because that's not what this question is pertaining to. Neither is this question centered around food nor being a glutton. On the contrary, this question is addressing fullness of love that a wife can provide her husband. Translating what is being asked, the question is, "Are you greedy for all of me – heart, body, and mind?" Men are no exception for disliking being used for one aspect of themselves. A hidden and rarely discussed revealing fact is that men, too, crave to be loved, appreciated, and respected for the totality of what they bring to the relationship table. In most cases, I believe it is safe to say that men reciprocate to their wives, at optimum performance across the board, when confident of their (wives) "greed" for them (as husbands). It's a wonderful experience to bask in the glory of being appreciatively greedy for one another.

Proverbs 5:18 (NLT): *Let your wife be a fountain of blessing for you. Rejoice in the wife of your youth.*

NOTE: Bear in mind C.A.T.

20. How long do you expect this relationship to last?

"I'm in it for the long haul."
"However long you'd like."

One of the best tools that a man, who is serious about a woman, can use to help both is the tool of advantageous conversation. This type of conversation centers around the purpose, benefit, and, most importantly, what's driving the duration of the relationship. Why it is advantageous for the woman is addressed in the section "Questions Women Do Not Ask Men but Should" (question #19)." It is advantageous for the man because for him to ask this question denotes that he's in focused mode and doesn't have time for play dating. He's ready and seeking to commit. He wants to carefully avoid wasting an unnecessary amount of time, effort, and resources on just anyone and save it for lavishing on that special deserving one. Yes, ladies! There are men who are sincerely willing and ready to settle down [in marriage] and give their all to the right woman at the right time without feeling pressured to do so.

Proverbs 3:27 (NLT): *Do not withhold good from those who deserve it when it's in your power to help them.*

NOTE: Bear in mind C.A.T.

21. Do you believe in monogamy?

"Depends on what my partner would agree to."

Not the response a man who's serious about a woman wants to hear. However, if you're in the top 99.9 percent of men, this is a question you certainly must ask. Today's relaxed and warped ideas and portrayals about commitments within relationships are reason enough to be concerned. No longer is it safe to assume that the woman of a man's dreams is or will be 100 percent committed solely to him. The lust of the flesh and overwhelming "reality" relationships depicted throughout various media outlets are vying strongly for her attention to engage in fallacious pleasures. As a man who is sincerely in search of a wife, surety of her integrity for a monogamous relationship must be clearly known. Finding out he has married an unfaithful wife is not something a man should stumble upon. The man must take the blinders off and ask before taking the leap that could turn his entire world upside down.

1 Corinthians 7:2 (NLT): *But because there is so much sexual immorality, each man should have his own wife, and each woman should have her own husband.*

NOTE: Bear in mind C.A.T.

22. What does "love" look like for you?

A correct but vague answer may be: "Love is shown by what we do for one another."

Some may accept and accentuate this as meaning the quantity and quality of material provision for one another; whereas others may express it more as how we treat each other. When a man asks this question, what is being sought is the woman's honest perception of love. This is key for the man in learning and comprehending the woman's love language, assessing whether he's able to measure up, and evaluating the connection between both of their perceptions about love – seeking a balanced connection. It would certainly befit a man to gain wisdom and understanding of love from God's perspective (using it to develop his character) prior to pursuing it based on the world's ideology. That way, when he's properly equipped to exude love, he's also properly equipped to recognize when it's genuinely being reciprocated from a woman of interest. Love means a lot of things to many people, but it can only be honestly and purely defined by the love giver.

1 Corinthians 13:4-7 (NLT): *Love is patient and kind. Love is not jealous or boastful or proud or rude. It does not demand its own way. It is not irritable, and it keeps no record of being wronged. It does not rejoice about injustice but rejoices whenever the truth*

wins out. Love never gives up, never loses faith, is always hopeful, and endures through every circumstance.

NOTE: Bear in mind C.A.T.

23. Do you have to like and be friends with your partner (because you sometimes do not have control of whom you fall in love with)?

"Not really, just go with the flow."

There are rare occasions when there is true mutual love at first sight soon followed by marriage without the two ever spending time to develop a relationship by becoming friends first. But in the "real" world, a man should not or is not going to marry a woman on a whim without first liking and being friends with her. The benefit of a man asking this question to a woman being considered for marriage is to make sure she's not settling for him. It's crucial that he knows the woman as his friend and that she not only likes but loves him. The friendship developed between the two is the difference-maker between like and love. Liking someone involves temporary tolerance whereas love is the unconditional and whole acceptance of one another – enjoying one another's company and character, sharing ideas, and overlooking quirky flaws. A man may not sometimes have control of whom he falls in love with, but he can guarantee that woman is his best friend, which makes the outlook of life's journey more promising.

Amos 3:3 (NLT): *Can two people walk together without agreeing on the direction?*

NOTE: Bear in mind C.A.T.

24. What are the lessons learned in our marriage?

"Not to ever do this again."

That's an answer from someone in a disturbed marriage. With the percentage of American marriages ending in divorce (hoovering between 40%-50%), it is a great idea for men to occasionally sit with their wives and discuss lessons learned in their marriage. A man taking the initiative for such a discussion will speak volumes to the wife's heart – once she's resuscitated from the surprise notion of him wanting to hold a conversation. All kidding aside, a man taking time to do this illustrates his commitment to the relationship and openness to make whatever necessary adjustments for making the relationship better, as likewise expected from the woman. It also presents the opportunity for gauging plans of the past in comparison to where the marriage and joint goals are now. Marriage-related lessons learned outfit both (husband and wife) with the tool of wisdom needed for bringing clarity to the vision to which they both agree, would like to have and are willing to work toward.

Proverbs 3:13 (NLT): *Joyful is the person who finds wisdom, the one who gains understanding.*

NOTE: Bear in mind C.A.T.

25. How do we grow spiritually and emotionally?

"By going with the flow and allowing everything to fall in place."

If it were that easy, there probably would be a far smaller divorce rate than what there currently is. This question helps to reveal a woman's level of spirituality [i.e., basis of her standards) and emotional needs [i.e., what motivates her emotionally]. Countless men jump into relationships with women based on them liking what they see, arbitrarily believing they can tolerate anything unknown about the woman. Not a good idea, as I'm sure that many of those very men can attest. It is essential for a man to know the woman's spiritual beliefs and emotional needs. This allows for him to make a clear conscious decision on whether they can operate and move forward as one [i.e., married], growing spiritually and emotionally. If so, it reveals how he can effectively assist in enhancing her spiritual life and fulfilling her emotional needs. In doing so, their shared faith must serve as the foundation.

Spirituality serves as the moral compass for what is considered acceptable and non-acceptable. Without it, a man becomes like a sailboat without a sail – ever off course and unable to meet any woman's emotional needs. What can be equally challenging is marrying a woman with a total opposite spiritual belief system or no spiritual belief at all. To alleviate the heartaches and pains, it is best to make it a point of having this discussion prior to marriage. If already married and on the same page, spiritual and emotional growth are inevitable when their prayers are committed to the Lord and biblical guidance/counsel is heeded.

Proverbs 16:3 (NLT): *Commit your actions to the LORD, and your plans will succeed.*

NOTE: Bear in mind C.A.T.

26. How do you feel about investment and risk management?

"Let's talk and do what we need to do."

Music to a man's ears. Men are prone to strategize for attaining financial freedom and stability. That being the case, a man asking a woman this question produces a hopeful two-fold result: 1) obtaining a generalized idea of her knowledge and how she feels about investment and risk management, and 2) petitioning her intellect for fresh ideas about the subject matter. Most people are aware and can agree that women are better financial managers. A man finding such a woman is well equipped with the key [i.e., her] to both their successes as one (in marriage) through exercising self-discipline and commitment to the goal. If the hopeful two-fold results are not realized, this discussion can still serve as a useful financial foundation for understanding the gamut of expectations and limitations from both party's perspectives. Afterward, a wise determination of either progressing forward as one or separately can be made without regret.

Proverbs 29:18 (NIV): *Where there is no revelation, people cast off restraint; but blessed is the one who heeds wisdom's instruction.*

NOTE: Bear in mind C.A.T.

27. What are your short- and long-term goals, and what are you actively doing to achieve them?

"Rest and more rest!"

Uh, no! Men thrive and are inspired by knowing what they're working with and what the goals are. Having a wife that gets it and works alongside him toward the goal(s) makes life even more grand and appreciated. It is assertively important for a man to build and witness symbols of progression. He must feel that what is being done is not in vain because he sees the work as an extension of himself [i.e., a fulfilled purpose]. Understandably, it's befuddling and aggravating for him to pull his weight [i.e., giving his all toward a shared goal] and have a spouse adding to that weight by not pulling her weight – especially when the plan has plainly been laid out and she's been equipped with time, materials, and opportunity to do her share of what needs to be done. To him, laziness is never an acceptable excuse for waste and could lead to him harboring emotional regrets that may very well lead to a relationship dissolvement.

Proverbs 20:13 (NIV): *Do not love sleep or you will grow poor; stay awake and you will have food to spare.*

NOTE: Bear in mind C.A.T.

28. How many kids do you foresee in your future?

"I'm too fine and having too much fun to ever consider talking about having kids."

Though it may not be the answer a potential father is looking for, it is one that is respected. Being in a relationship, each partner has their idea of whether children are in their future; hence, why it is vital to have this discussion upfront when in a serious relationship. Men see children as an extension of himself, carrying on the name and heritage of him and his ancestors, likewise true for the woman. The discussion should further extend into areas of whether the woman is able to have children, possibilities of adopting, financial status to support an entire family, etc. On the flip side of the coin, there are men who simply can't fathom bringing children into this world, not even through adoption, because of fears, stresses, finances, or selfishness. Regardless of the reason for or against having children in the future, each man needs to be linked with a like-minded woman.

Psalm 127:3 (NLT): *Children are a gift from the LORD; they are a reward from him.*

NOTE: Bear in mind C.A.T.

29. Where would you like to live?

"Wherever you'd like."

A life-changing decision doesn't and shouldn't solely lie in what the man thinks or likes. Lasting marital relationships are built with fruitful compromises for the benefit of both people. A man and woman both providing input to where they'd like to live equips them for making a well-informed joint decision that fairly appeases them both. It also ushers in further discussion points for them to jointly consider such as: employment opportunities, preferred weather climates, schooling for children, crime statistics, cost of living, taxes, etc. Something else that is a worthwhile consideration would be geographic distance from family members. As much as men try to distance themselves in proximity from family, God forbid if something were to happen to either partner.

When searching for that final [i.e., retirement] home, the entire family matters. Lastly, for a woman to not have profitable input on home locale is unwise. The man is asking because he values her opinion and sees her as an equal partner.

Proverbs 13:16 (NLT): *A wise woman builds her home, but a foolish woman tears it down with her own hands.*

NOTE: Bear in mind C.A.T.

30. Are you interested in owning a home or renting?

"I'm fine living in a box as long as we're in there together."

As sweet as it sounds, it's not the response a man seeks. Generally, if a man is asking this question, he's fishing for hints of affordability and possibly a deeper conversation of clarity regarding her contributions. The last thing he wants is for her to dream, plan, and 'live big' based primarily on his finances, with her bringing little to nothing to the table. The answer to this question helps him to avoid being trapped struggling to pay for something he can't afford alone. Additionally, depending on her answer and them being married, they may want to consider renting before making the major decision of purchasing a home. Renting will allow the couple time to work out faulty housekeeping habits and financial kinks as well as get a feel for the size of home that would be manageable and accommodating to their needs. Maintaining open communication and having an effective partnership is the setup for successfully owning a home.

Proverbs 22:26-27 (NIV): *Do not be one who shakes hands in pledge or puts up security for debts; if you lack the means to pay, your very bed will be snatched from under you.*

NOTE: Bear in mind C.A.T.

31. How should we manage our money?

"With an understanding."

That's a response a man couldn't agree more with. In marriage, part of becoming one includes a merging of finances. A lot of men don't consider that concept while dating but the idea becomes very real when going into marriage, which is why it is important to ask this question and discuss it upfront. In marriage, it cannot be a "what's mine is mine" type deal for either party. Again, therefore a man must realize that he has important financial decisions to make before marriage, with the biggest being can he really trust the woman whom he loves so dearly? Most people know that a man's validation is tied to his money; hence, why he loves flaunting and spending it on that special woman in his life. However, marriage calls for having financial discipline and a new realm of responsibilities to include establishing spending priorities.

It is always a great idea to have individual spending accounts as well as joint savings (for vacations, gifts, etc.) and checking accounts (for paying bills/living expenses). However, it is essential to have the element of trust between both partners so that either a will or power of attorney can be drafted designating the other as beneficiary to the individual spending accounts (in case of emergency only – i.e., death, etc.). Finally, when a man speaks his peace during the discussion on this topic, Women, please listen carefully and know that he will hold you accountable to whatever is agreed upon.

Matthew 25:20-21 (NLT): *The servant to whom he had entrusted the five bags of silver came forward with five more and said, 'Master, you gave me five bags of silver to invest, and I have earned five more.' "The master was full of praise. 'Well done, my good and faithful servant. You have been faithful in handling this small amount, so now I will give you many more responsibilities. Let's celebrate together!'*

NOTE: Bear in mind C.A.T.

32. Have you had any financial hardships I need to know about?

"Not really, I just trash the bills and change where I live."

Logically the man should take that answer to be a resounding "YES!" Financial hardships will end a relationship quicker than love started it. Men typically like to be the saving grace whom a woman can depend on for anything. However, a man linking up with a woman experiencing financial hardships is not very wise. He should consider there being a high probability of her having bad spending habits as well as illiteracy about finances that she's accustomed to and will surely bring into the relationship. Once married, those problems become shared problems with which it becomes difficult to cut ties, costing much more than he may have bargained for.

Proverbs 17:18 (NLT): *It's poor judgment to guarantee another person's debt or put up security for a friend.*

NOTE: Bear in mind C.A.T.

33. Do you find this to be a true statement, "If your car is nasty then so are your home and bodily hygiene?" If so, does it pertain to you?

"I see no reason for answering this if we love each other."

Using the term "love" loosely is one thing, but for a man to tolerate what he considers a pet peeve is something entirely different. For the record, when it comes to cleanliness there are a lot of men who are very observant about a woman's upkeep of self, vehicle, and dwelling. If any flaws are detected in the upkeep of either, it generally becomes a deal breaker for the man. Although she may be thinking, acting on, and talking the language of love, he has already made up in his mind that she is only a temporary date being used for passing time. At the serious relationship scouting phase of a man's life, this question is necessary because he's not looking to marry a woman who sees nothing wrong with being disorganized. That type of attitude symbolizes to him that if he moves forward in marriage with this woman, he now has another job on his hand – that's a weight of unwelcomed stress that he can do without. She may possess high intelligence, a go-getter spirit, and great looks and conversation; however, those attributes along with hygiene are the keys to the heart of many men.

1 Corinthians 14:40 (NLT): *But be sure that everything is done properly and in order.*

NOTE: Bear in mind C.A.T.

34. Do you believe in God, and what are your thoughts on religion?

"I go to church at times but I'm not all that into religion."

Sadly, we're living in a moment of time when this is the response of far too many people. When God isn't a priority, there really aren't any moral standards nor place for accountability in one's life. As men, it is especially important to know God beyond casually and to have a personal, intimate relationship with him. It's in that relationship with God that a man can be equipped for making wise, beneficial, and appropriate life decisions. With marriage being one of those life decisions, he will need to be accessible to the spirit of God guiding him with discernment to the woman who's specifically prepared for him. The godly man and woman will be like-minded and, most importantly, have the word of God to prosperously govern them, their marriage, their children, and their shared life's journey. If the woman he's dating doesn't have time for God or so called "religion", he should take heed. If she does believe in God and religion, it will be to his benefit that he prays about it and remains open for discernment from God – He will either confirm or disprove in some form or another, which will bring peace.

Psalm 14:1 (NIV): *The fool says in his heart, "There is no God." They are corrupt, their deeds are vile; there is no one who does good.*

NOTE: Bear in mind C.A.T.

35. If you could go back in time and change anything, what would you change and why?

"I'd change personal regrets."

Posing this question to a woman assists a man in knowing whether she is living in the past, negatively affected by the past, and/or needs professional help [i.e., mental health treatment] to escape the past. Yes, there are devasting situations that women have had and continue to endure, which makes it difficult to simply forget and move on as though nothing happened. With that in mind, a man must be willing to sit, listen and understand her expressed past regrets without casting judgement. A word of encouragement may be sharing how a start for changing the past is by taking advantage of the grace provided today. Help her understand that today (the present) is the day when she can choose to progress beyond what yesterday was. There are massive amounts of available opportunities, resources, and programs that provide support for dealing with various past regrets. The past has passed and the only value it can bring to the here and now is knowing it was used to get all of us where we are today. A man should let her know how the past was a steppingstone to get her to him.

Philippians 3:13-14 (NLT): *No, dear brothers and sisters, I have not achieved it, but I focus on this one thing: Forgetting the past and looking forward to what lies ahead, I press on to reach the end of the race and receive the heavenly prize for which God, through Christ Jesus, is calling us.*

NOTE: Bear in mind C.A.T.

Questions Men Do Not Ask Women but Should

36. What would I miss out on if I don't choose you as a spouse?

"All this!"

Hopefully she would go on to specifically define what "all this" means. It is very helpful for a man to realize what sets the woman (potential wife) he's with apart from any other woman. Yes, he has his own perceptional reasons for being with her, but a man doesn't want what he thinks and says about her to be the motivation nor the foundation of her self-esteem. This is an opportunity for her to modestly talk about what she brings to the relationship—make known the value of who she is—and how she sees and feels about herself. Men-scoundrels look for women whose esteem is built on what they say about them. Real men look for and marry women who respectfully know their self-worth and are not willing to compromise for anyone. A woman whose actions, character, and confidence are above reproach is a woman for whom a real man would go to the moon.

Proverbs 31:10 (NLT): *Who can find a virtuous and capable wife? She is more precious than rubies.*

NOTE: Bear in mind C.A.T.

37. How do you feel about being a stepparent?

"I'm fine with it as long as they're not disrespectful."

Unfortunately, there are many women who will claim to be fine with the idea of being a stepparent but when realization sets in it becomes a totally different story, especially if she's bringing children of her own into the relationship. There are women who find it difficult separating stepchildren from their thoughts and emotions about the biological mothers. Suddenly they begin viewing the children as mere by-products of a failed relationship, considering themselves (and their own biological children) as the prize. With it being a constant hurdle for them (women) to overcome, they're easily prone to mistreating the innocent children.

A quick way for a woman to lose hopes of marriage to a man she loves is her shunning his children. Most participatory, good fathers will find it completely unacceptable and drop the axe immediately. A warning for fathers is to not assume that because she's a woman and/or a mother that she automatically shares your affections and will have your children's best interest at heart. Observe her interactions beyond what she says, have conversations with your children, and most importantly, wisely listen and investigate what their (your children's) concerns are as they relay them to you.

Proverbs 14:1 (NIV): *The wise woman builds her house, but with her own hands the foolish one tears hers down.*

NOTE: Bear in mind C.A.T.

38. Have you ever been arrested for domestic abuse?

"I've been given a warning but never arrested."

Take that response as a warning. There is a prevalent untruth that only women can be or are victims of domestic abuse. Truth be known, domestic abuse shows no victim partiality. Men beware that strength is not exhibited by accepting abuse from a woman, it's being able to not tolerate and shut the door on such a relationship before getting deeply involved. Pure love is not defined in abusive behavior (verbally, psychologically, or physically). One telltale sign can be observed in how she reacts when something doesn't go how she believes it should. Listen to her verbal language, beware of her guilt trips, and look for stubbornness. If she lacks patience and understanding, it will be uncovered. If the relationship starts out with the man being passive on any inclinations and/or forms of abuse, once married it will gradually worsen. A man should look beyond what he thinks he can change about a woman because in the end that change will negatively be manifested in him.

Proverbs 22:24-25 (NIV): *Do not make friends with a hot-tempered person, do not associate with one easily angered, or you may learn their ways and get yourself ensnared.*

NOTE: Bear in mind C.A.T.

39. Have you ever attended job corps?

"That's a weird question, why do you ask?"

A response you are sure to get. The reasoning behind this question is to increase honesty and gather hidden background information used for knowing the woman he is considering becoming his wife. It may be a weird question for a woman who hasn't been to job corps but it's an intriguing question for the one who has. She may have her reason(s) for not revealing it to the man sooner; however, by him asking this question it lessens any reservation and shame she may have as well as his willingness to discuss the intricacies of her ups and downs, known and unknown encourages her emotionally. This is man's way of showing how he is ready and prepared to accept all that made and makes her who she is. Many uninformed people view job corps in a negative light. On the contrary, it is simply another method/institution used to educate and train young individuals – it is an opportunity worth seizing for the young adults needing guidance in getting on track in life. This man cares about this woman!

Philippians 3:15-16 (NLT): *But we must hold on to the progress we have already made.*

NOTE: Bear in mind C.A.T.

40. What is your highest level of education?

"No need to ask that, I'm smart enough to figure out whatever."

Are you really? It goes without saying but at times needs repeating, 'Education is fundamental'. A man generally seeks a woman who is at least on the same educational and common-sense level or more highly intelligent than he. Though there are dire exceptions to why some haven't completed the normal education grades (K-12), for many women who have had the opportunity and decided to quit before graduation, it speaks volumes to a man. He's looking long-term with thought-provoking questions such as: How will this woman be able to help with our children's educational needs [i.e., homework, etc.]? How will she be able to comprehend simple directions? How will she be able to interact with VIP persons?

How can I depend on her to handle important matters relating to finances, bills, etc.? Though neither of these questions suggests that education is needed for a woman to know how to accomplish these tasks, it does not negate how level of education and common sense are realities of concern for what he seeks in a woman. With love one can work through anything, but without some form of education and common sense, one is limited in what can be handled.

Proverbs 24:10 (NLV): *If you are weak in the day of trouble, your strength is small.*

NOTE: Bear in mind C.A.T.

41. What are your expectations of this union?

"Can we set aside an entire week to discuss?"

Take that as a positive response. Men who are willing to discuss expectations of a union with their partner, fiancée or wife are men who are ready to surely grow. One of the worse decisions a couple could ever make in a relationship is to never discuss expectations of one another as well as joint (ones). Operating based on assumptions within a relationship is likened to a train being stalled on the track due to having locomotives in front and the rear, both attempting to move in separate directions. It is very critical and beneficial for men to solicit a woman's expectations of their union while dating rather than finding something out later that he regrets not knowing sooner. He needs to know upfront whether she views the relationship the same as he does (short- and/or long-term) as well as a myriad of other relationship details. Never get caught up in what's working today while overlooking building a future for tomorrow.

Proverbs 31:25 (NLV): *Her clothes are strength and honor. She is full of joy about the future.*

NOTE: Bear in mind C.A.T.

42. Can you agree to a monthly conversation about aligning goals as we grow?

"I'm ready now, let's talk."

Women know how difficult it can be to get most men to open up, so they tend to seize the opportunity of conversing at a moment's notice. Men are known for keeping plans and goals locked within their minds, all the while expecting women to know what they're thinking. That is a setup for failure for any relationship. If and when a man proposes to have a conversation regarding aligning goals, he and she should be prepared for two actions. The first is her listening carefully as he provides his ideas and goals – on average men dislike repeating themselves. Secondly, he needs to exercise patience and be prepared to answer questions precisely – on average women are into details (receiving and giving information). The great news about a man asking this question is that it shows he has already envisioned having a bright future with the woman.

Proverbs 4:25 (NLT): *Look straight ahead, and fix your eyes on what lies before you.*

NOTE: Bear in mind C.A.T.

43. Is marriage something you truly want, or the perceived stability of it?

"For this present moment, I'd say both."

After that answer, a man can go ahead and call it a wrap and move on. This is a needful question primarily because of faulty ideas and shams for marrying today. Society, reality portrayals through various media outlets, and ulterior motives transform many women into great actors for getting what they want out of a man today. Some women forego marriage altogether and are very satisfied with just having a child with a man whom she can use for obtaining child-support all in the name of income security. Men must use common sense, listen to wise and trusted female family and friends, and utilize prayer along with the word of God to decipher the motives and realness of a woman he's interested in. Likewise, whatever her answer is to this question, run it by God in prayer, close trustworthy women [i.e., mother, sister, etc.], and research what is said about it in the Bible. Her answer could be a setup for her either being a blessing in your life or torture for the rest of your life.

Proverbs 31:3 (TMB): *Don't dilute your strength on fortune-hunting women, promiscuous women who shipwreck leaders.*

NOTE: Bear in mind C.A.T.

44. What are your expectations as a mother/wife?

"To be a mother and a wife."

After he scratches his head, (seriously) he may ask for another answer or (jokingly) assume the light isn't on and walk away. In all sincerity, he's in search of how the woman views being a mother and wife in efforts of sizing it up against his views. Some men like to be smothered by their wives, others not so much. Some men prefer their wives to take the lead tending to the children while others may want a joint effort. Some men want a wife and mother like their mothers and others may want the opposite. Without a doubt, every fiancé or married man desires a wife he can trust and who enhances his life. Whatever her expectations are, he is looking for that special woman who can come as close as possible to what his expectations are of her – the same can be said of her expectations of him as a husband and father. A man must know those expectations before making that forever commitment.

Proverbs 31:11 (NLT): *Her husband can trust her, and she will greatly enrich his life.*

NOTE: Bear in mind C.A.T.

45. Who comes first and why (spouse or children)?

"Why don't you answer that first?"

This is a sensitive topic for both parties. What a man wishes to know is the woman's concept regarding relationships between the two of them and between them and their children. A mature man posing this question is not asking nor expecting the woman to choose one over the other, rather he is wanting to know if she sees herself and him primarily as joint decision-making partners sharing responsibilities for nurturing and preparing the children to someday become responsible adults.

Mature men understand, accept, and appreciate a wife's love, care, and protection of their child(ren). He has bought into the concept of partnership in marriage and needs not to ever question his place in his wife's life. That is while the child is a child. However, when that child has become a young adult (graduate from 12th grade and/or college), it's time to cut the total support strings and allow that grown individual (especially male) to take flight. Rarely would a man aid the immaturity of an adult offspring by allowing the individual to idly lounge around their (husband & wife's) house without a job, not having any responsibilities and/or contributions.

From a logical standpoint, the man realizes it's not doing that adult son/daughter (especially son) any good, allowing them to live like a freeloading fatted calf. It will only lead to friction between he and his wife. With many women having a heart of compassion (expressly for their children), they typically have the patience and tendency to go out of the way for their adult offspring, treating them as though they're still little children. By doing so, the man and woman are no longer operating as one because she has now prioritized another ADULT above her marriage, which creates unneeded but warranted tensions within the marriage.

Pray and obtain professional and godly marriage counseling prior to marrying. It'll prevent ignorance from turning one another's love to hate.

Ephesians 5:21 (LB): *Honor Christ by submitting to each other.*
Ephesians 5:33 (NLT): *So again I say, each man must love his wife as he loves himself, and the wife must respect her husband.*

Ephesians 6:1 (LB): *Children, obey your parents; this is the right thing to do because God has placed them in authority over you.*

NOTE: Bear in mind C.A.T.

46. What are you passionate about?

"Showing love."

Such a vague answer that can either be good or bad. Good in that maybe she knows how to love, and bad that she may be speaking from the standpoint of being an addict to something not good. Seriously speaking, contrary to popular belief, there are many men who would love to have a woman who's filled with promising passions for positive factors such as life, career, family, hobbies, vacations, etc. As a matter of fact, the primary reason a man would like to know what she's passionate about is for discovering like passions they probably share. Learning the passions of a woman he loves ignites a feeling of excitement for him in that it presents a challenge for him to further connect with her. For a caring man, being mindful of her passions is the tool needed for him to spontaneously plan special events or give ideal gifts that he knows will please her. It delights a man greatly to know that he's with a woman who is driven by passion and even more so if it's a shared passion of interest.

Proverbs 31:13 (MEV): *She seeks wool and flax, and works willingly with her hands.*

NOTE: Bear in mind C.A.T.

47. Were you ever abused and, if so, by who?

"I prefer not to talk about it."

Though she may not want to talk about it, the man who's seriously considering marrying such a woman must be patient and handle the situation delicately in getting her to open up for discussion. There are a lot of hidden personal traumas that both sexes experience which becomes the driving force of certain behavior they may exhibit. It is important for this discussion to happen primarily so that the man knows the safe and danger zones regarding what triggers her emotions, thoughts, and behavior during disagreements, interactions with certain people, etc. His having the knowledge of past abuse is not to **ever** be used as a weapon against her. It is to provide assurance of love, support, protection, and to prevent any egregious abuse(s) from occurring again. Furthermore, it aids him in helping her have a life of self-control rather than possibly unexplainable and damaging outbursts of wrath. A man who's willing to love beyond and walk with a woman through a troubling past is a godsend.

Proverbs 14:29 (NLT): *People with understanding control their anger, a hot temper shows great foolishness.*

NOTE: Bear in mind C.A.T.

48. Would you consider seeing a mental health professional if advised or needed?

"Will you?"

Such a defense signifies her answer of "NO!" We are in an age where we have come a long way medically, all for the good. We now have resources and specialists to help us deal with unlimited specific mental health issues. A man who asks this question is not only caring but wise. He wants to know if she's willing to step outside the box in seeking wise and professional counseling if needed. Not only that, but he's also evaluating whether she can be supportive and/or trusted if he's the one needing to consult with a mental health professional – not a woman who will shun or view him as weak. There are many unwise men who would allow a personal mental health issue to destroy their very beings and marriages for the sake of pride. Maintaining pride is not worth sacrificing mental peace. For mental health to be a concern and asked about from a man, he's looking to have a long and peaceful life with a special kind of woman.

Proverbs 12:15 (LB): *A fool thinks he needs no advice, but a wise man listens to others.*

NOTE: Bear in mind C.A.T.

49. Are you saving for retirement?

"That's what social security is for, so no."

This is a typical and imprudent response from many who ignorantly haven't considered the totality of financial facts and needs for retirement years [i.e., old age]. The answer to this question predicts a financial starting point with a potential bride. A man will either link with a woman building upon their resources or struggling to maintain and build upon his resources. There are those who have a retirement account along with other investments and an operative plan with a vision. Then there are those who function in life with a vision of finding and marrying such a person – bringing no retirement plan nor financial contributions to the relationship. It would be foolish for a man to partner with a woman for life who's without some level of financial intellect, discipline, and resources. Although no one is promised tomorrow it doesn't negate planning for it – if not for you, think about your spouse and/or children.

Proverbs 10:15 (NLT): *The wealth of the rich is their fortress; the poverty of the poor is their destruction.*

NOTE: Bear in mind C.A.T.

50. Do you communicate (i.e., text, talk, meet for lunch, etc.) on a regular basis with people you are attracted to?

"Maybe. I haven't given it much thought."

As soon as a man hears that type of answer, he's already thinking, "yeah, right!" Yes, men and women can have platonic relationships and keep it as just that. However, it's an entirely different story for a man to be with a woman who's maintaining regular contact with someone she's discreetly attracted to. She may not (most cases will not) verbally relay to her partner about her attraction toward another man but know for certain, his intuition is at work. Intuition is a gift we each possess and have a choice to ignore or question/act upon. Most men who intuitively discern his partner's attraction and/or affection for another man, will confront the issue on the spot (the results probably won't be too promising for a future together if she's defending why she should continue communicating with the person). When a man solicits his female companion with this question, depending on her response, it will either be his reason for severing the relationship or continuing into marriage. He's seeking a woman who has cut those ties (just as he should have) and is ready to live a new life solely committed to him as he is to her. He has no patience or time to waste on wondering about shadiness.

2 Corinthian 5:17 (NLT): *This means that anyone who belongs to Christ has become a new person. The old life is gone; a new life has begun!*

NOTE: Bear in mind C.A.T.

51. Are you still intimately involved with your ex?

"What do you think?"

At that point, he will probably say something to the effect of, "I don't know, that's why I asked!" This is definitely a need-to-ask pre-date question. All too often, lives are lost and relationships are destroyed because of deceptive statements of supposed ex-partners being out of a woman's life. If the man has any inclination of ties between the woman and her ex (beyond shared children), it will benefit him to sever his ties with her and move on to a brighter pasture. If the ex is really out of the picture and she's sincere about being in a relationship with the new man, the new man needs to know without a doubt that it is just he and her. Beware, hidden intimacy with a past partner while in a new relationship will only produce devastating consequences.

Proverbs 7:25-27 (NLT): *Don't let your hearts stray away toward her. Don't wander down her wayward path. For she has been the ruin of many: many men have been her victims. Her house is the road to the grave. Her bedroom is the den of death.*

NOTE: Bear in mind C.A.T.

52. What major trauma(s) have you experienced and are still dealing with?

"I have been diagnosed with post-traumatic stress disorder resulting from…"

This question is in no way intended for casting judgment. Rather, it is for awareness and discussion of how a man (partner) can assist and/or further understand the woman (wife to be) through knowledge of any traumatic incident she's experienced. Her candidness to this discussion presents a form of intimate bonding with the man. Intimacy within a relationship doesn't start and end with sex. Intimacy is a shared culmination of past, present, future, good and bad, rights and wrongs, failures and successes, etc. It is love put forth in an effort to know your partner to a degree greater than anyone else can, has, or will. It's providing support whether needed or not. Most importantly, it's praying for one another and realizing you are both the answer God has delivered into each of your lives. A man's heart is demonstrated by doing all he can to make life comfortable and pleasing for his wife. His devoted care for her is God's blessing in action.

1 Peter 5:7 (NLT): *Give all your worries and cares to God, for he cares about you.*

NOTE: Bear in mind C.A.T.

53. What's your stance on forgiveness?

"I may forgive but I will not forget!"

This is not a question he is asking because he's planning to do something that would require her forgiveness and he wants to know the consequences upfront. This question is mainly meant to identify any lingering hang-ups she may have due to unforgiveness. It's a terrible situation for a man to find himself dating a woman who is continually stuck in the past about how another man (or men) has cheated, lied, stole, etc. while with her. It's difficult to grow in such a relationship when she is constantly questioning and comparing everything the current man does based on what was done in the past. She may be a great woman in many ways but her harboring unforgiveness is something hard to contend with. Before a man moves forward with this type of woman, it is strongly advised that both get wise and professional counseling. Without counseling, he will find himself either passing on what could've been an incredible woman or marrying a very untrusting, bitter woman, which in turn leads to an untrusting, bitter marriage full of regrets.

Ephesians 4:31-32 (NLT): *Get rid of all bitterness, rage, anger, harsh words, and slander, as well as all types of evil behavior. Instead, be kind to each other, tenderhearted, forgiving one another, just as God through Christ has forgiven you.*

NOTE: Bear in mind C.A.T.

54. Can you occasionally spoil me at times (i.e., take me out for dinner, shopping, pedicure, etc. just because)?

"Of course, if you're paying."

Such an answer warrants an equally facetious rebuttal: "Bye!" All kidding aside, relationships are based on compromise, a give and take mutual respect. After all, if both have jobs and bringing income to the table, what problem should she have in spoiling the man at times? If she's stingy or sees no reason to do so, that is a cause for concern. The relationship can't nor should be one-way, in that he gives, and she takes. If it's all about what he can do for her, that is selfish thinking on her part that needs to be resolved immediately. He's not asking to be spoiled at every turn, just spontaneously at times.

Understandably, there are men who consider it belittling or unchivalrous for a woman to "spoil" them. They rather keep the pressure on themselves for being the romantic stud for the sake of feeling like a "man." On the other hand, if the man couldn't care less or does not want his partner spoiling him, he will be responsible for one of two developments: 1) validating her stingy behavior, or 2) her having to suppress her appreciation of him. Men, read this carefully: "Her spoiling you doesn't make you any less of a man." She's your partner not your enemy! Allow her the opportunity to shower you with appreciation. Men, know what you're looking for in a woman and don't stifle the blessing she brings.

Proverbs 31:12 (MSG): *Never spiteful, she treats him generously all her life long.*

NOTE: Bear in mind C.A.T.

55. How often are you willing to have sex?

"We'll see."

This is the one question that many relationships are heavily built on. The problem with men asking this is that they're typically thinking and measuring their appetite based on the present without giving any thought about future stamina or health issues. In such cases, men, be careful of what you lust [i.e., ask] for – you could be in for more than you think you're prepared for. Onward, without a doubt, sex plays a major role in marriage hence why it needs to and should be discussed in-depth between the man and woman. There should be respect and understanding for the need as well as the timing and/or amount of sex within marriage. On average, as men get older there comes a decrease in sexual stamina whereas women experience an increase. In either case, both sexual drives should be reasonably accommodated by both parties as much as possible. Lastly, let not sex serve as the foundation of the marriage in place of unconditional love. For sure, it will take love to get through everything when sex fails.

1 Corinthians 7:5 (NIV): *Do not deprive each other except perhaps by mutual consent and for a time, so that you may devote yourselves to prayer. Then come together again so that Satan will not tempt you because of your lack of self-control.*

NOTE: Bear in mind C.A.T.

56. Whom would you compare my qualities as a man to?

"Probably more like my ex."

A definite wrong answer! No man wants to be compared to his partner's ex in any way. Now back to reality. The reasoning for this question is for a man to gather subliminal information on how his partner views him based on her admiration of the man or men she names. Men must keep in mind that her answer is founded on her innocent, characteristic observations of him and other men. In no way should a man use her answer as an indication of her wanting him to be more like someone else. On the contrary, she's with him out of sheer appreciation of who he is just as he's with her for the same reason. Can men use tweaking in certain qualities? Certainly! A few advantages of her answer is that it shines light on how he may be viewed by others (positive or negative), opens the door for discussion on what and how he can be better, and can be used to affirm whether he's on track with pleasing her by how he treats and represents her.

Proverbs 22:1 (NIV): *A good name is more desirable than great riches; to be esteemed is better than silver or gold.*

NOTE: Bear in mind C.A.T.

57. When was your last relationship and why did it end?

"About a month ago. It ended because we drifted apart."

For a man, this should be one of the top five upfront questions to ask a woman of interest. Knowing when and the reason behind her last relationship ending provides insight into her extent of commitment to a relationship. In most cases, every relationship starts with both being in "love", that is until something or someone else (including self) becomes the priority. For a man to truly love a woman, there has to be an emotional breakthrough for him that bonds him with her. On the norm, women are used to the power of emotions, however for many men, it is like a new world experience. Once his emotions are tapped into and he begins expressing his love for and to the woman, in his mind, the relationship is considered the same as a marriage. For this reason, it is imperative for a man to ask, discuss, and ensure she's ready for what he's prepared to sacrifice (i.e., his emotions, time, efforts, and resources) for the sake of a relationship leading to marriage.

Proverbs 25:19 (NLT): *Putting confidence in an unreliable person in times of trouble is like chewing with a broken tooth or walking on a lame foot.*

NOTE: Bear in mind C.A.T.

58. What's your take on current matters in the world?

"I'm all about positive energy, I have no time for the negative in the world."

That answer suffices for someone who's fine living in a box with blinders on. A lot of men, on a broader perspective, are news-oriented. Men regularly stay and engage in-the-know of the world, basically because of their nature of being planners and fixers. They rely on the news to help prepare for what's outside the doors of their home daily, economy updates, what to expect tomorrow, and cautions for living. Living a fruitful life involves staying abreast, not being consumed in fear or living trapped in a bubble. Many opportunities are missed due to lack of knowledge regarding current matters.

Oppositely and interestingly, there are many couples who have split because of disagreements about what each supports based on current matters in the world. If there's something that either the man or woman simply can't compromise on, they have a choice for either staying clear of that particular topic [i.e., agree to disagree] or relieving themselves from the relationship. It would be advantageous for both parties to discuss and iron out the differences during the dating phase rather than making later attempts in marriage. A man who takes extreme interest in current world matters must be careful to not allow those views to cause a dissention in his relationship with his partner. Finally, mutual respect must be given toward one another's views on current matters of the world.

1 Peter 5:8 (NIV): *Be alert and of sober mind. Your enemy the devil prowls around like a roaring lion looking for someone to devour.*

NOTE: Bear in mind C.A.T.

Questions Women Do Not Ask Men but Should

Questions
Women Do Not Ask Men
but Should

1. What's your idea of a woman?

"A ride or die partner!"
"Someone who takes care of the home (i.e., cook, clean, children, etc.)"

Firstly, a ride or die partner should only be in marriage seeing that's a huge cost of loyalty to pay a man who doesn't think enough of a woman to legally make a commitment. Secondly, society has come a long way from the archaic days of confining women to the home, neglecting her welfare for the sake of pleasing a man. If a man explains his idea of a woman with either statement, he's either selfish or ignorant and in desperate need of enlightenment.

This question is ideal for a woman to ask a man for understanding how he may view her. His answer paints a picture from his perspective and it's up to the woman to determine whether she sees herself in the portrait or chooses not to be a part of it. She must not allow herself to be wooed by his answer, leading to an attempt to become what he's looking for. During his answering, it is to her advantage to intelligently gather information on what type of man he is based on how he views women. Such information equips her in making an intelligent decision to either invest forward in the relationship or save a lot of time, effort, and possible heartache by severing the relationship (or possibility of there being one).

What no woman should do is falsely fit into a man's idea of a woman out of infatuation. Doing so only sets her up for hearing those words that any woman would dread to hear from a man, "I don't want you!" It can't be emphasized enough but it is very vital for a woman to recognize and realize that it's okay to not measure up to his idea of a woman; it is more important that she not under- or oversell being who she is. A man's idea is not meant to define the absolute woman, it's just his opinion based on either how well educated he is about women or his thoughts of what he's looking for in a woman. Either she fits the mold, decides whether she's willing and able to make any adjustments, or sees it as a relationship that's not worth the investment.

Proverbs 31:10 (NLT): *Who can find a virtuous and capable wife? She is more precious than rubies.*

NOTE: Bear in mind C.A.T.

2. Have you ever womanized?

"If you're asking have I ever been with another woman, the answer is yes."

That's considered to be a snowball answer being thrown (out of fear) at the woman to minimize his involvements with multiple women and to get her to move on to another topic. He fears being exposed so he provides a generic male-programmed answer. A woman should be insistent on a man answering this question fully and honestly. If he's providing any inclination of shade to divert, beware and stay clear. There is no marriage potential to be found in a womanizer – it's what he does and who he is. No woman has the power, love, looks, or sex to change who and what he is. It is a matter of the heart between that man and God.

While it is true that a man can change, it would be in a woman's best interest to trust but verify by discreetly investigating such change through casual talks with trusted friends, family, and associates. A woman who is confident in her faith, herself, and her worth will soon come across a man who realizes and treats her as the gift she is.

Matthew 10:16 (NLV): *I am sending you out like sheep with wolves all around you. Be wise like snakes and gentle like doves.*

NOTE: Bear in mind C.A.T.

3. Have you ever treated women poorly (not abusive)?

"Depends on what you mean by that. I treat them how they treat me."

This type of answer signifies the man's immaturity and childlike behavior. The answer a woman is seeking is a simple "yes" (which will lead to further discussion) or "no". There is a saying which goes, "observe how he treats his mother and/or sister and you'll know what to expect in his treatment of you." Sounds good but not an absolute truth. There are men who hold their mother and/or sister at much higher esteem than they ever would any woman (including their wives). Although it's advantageous to observe a man's interactions with the women he respects most in his life, it's more important to observe how he treats the woman of interest in private and in public as well. If there's a contradiction of behavior in any way, a woman should heed her intuition, discuss the issue with the man, and, if she's adamant about moving forward in a relationship with him, definitely seek professional counseling. If his intent is to marry the woman, his love for her will be consistent and immeasurably evident in private and in public.

Proverbs 26:11 (NLT): *As a dog returns to its vomit, so a fool repeats his foolishness.*

NOTE: Bear in mind C.A.T.

4. How does your upbringing shape your attitude about money?

"By keeping me on the grind to get what I can."

When a woman asks a man this question, it's to gauge his intelligence and maturity level about finances. It's imperative for her to know whether he's a planner, careless spender, and/or giver. His answer becomes the tool needed for her vision of how life would be with him, which affords her the opportunity to make a wise decision about continuing a relationship with such a person. His upbringing may have strongly and wrongly influenced his attitude about money or it may have done quite the opposite. At the same time, she must consider her own attitude about money and make sure she's being responsible and/or willing to make necessary adjustments just as she's expecting of him. It would be wise for her to partner with a man who is equally open and willing to change, being like-minded with hope about their financial future. Both should be agreeable to practicing financial discipline and management by building beyond yesteryears' limited knowledge – having one another's best interest at heart for a prosperous life together.

Proverbs 14:1 (NIV): *The wise woman builds her house, but with her own hands the foolish one [woman] tears hers down.*

NOTE: Bear in mind C.A.T.

5. What are your spending priorities?

"Showering you with whatever you want and need as well as getting me that new all electric Bentley."

Right off the bat, a woman should pick up quickly on the immaturity in this shallow statement. Asking this question presents a woman the opportunity of knowing what he considers a priority [i.e., living for today, impressing others, a stable future, etc.]. A man who spends haphazardly or considers showering a woman and himself with expensive gifts (especially with use of credit) is a financially uneducated, irresponsible, and foolish man. A few factors a woman should either look for in a man's response or bring up for discussion about spending are his honoring God in his finances [i.e., giving to church, charitable organizations, etc.], how he handles financial obligations [i.e., bills, loans, etc.], his thoughts and actions about investing, his thoughts about financially planning with a spouse, and how much image [i.e., what others think] influences his spending.

When a woman asks about a man's spending priorities, she's looking for that potential mate who not only respects financial responsibilities but also who is self-disciplined and not too materialistic. Discussing spending priorities is very important for both parties who are seriously seeking a married life together and it warrants discussion prior to marriage.

For believers, the priority of spending should begin by both of you spending time with God in prayer and in His word. From there, the priority of spending your financial resources should be dedicating an established percentage to your place of worship followed by however you both agree and deem as most to least significant in building financial security as one.

Proverbs 3:9-10 (AMP): *Honor the LORD with your wealth and with the first fruits of all your crops (income); then your barns will be abundantly filled and your vats will overflow with new wine.*

NOTE: Bear in mind C.A.T.

6. When do you plan to retire and how will you afford it?

"Once I get a job, I'll think about that."
"I don't."

Those are just a couple of answers a woman can expect from a lazy man or workaholic. There is a balance in life, a time to work and a time to relax. Such balance comes by wisdom and understanding. Whereas a woman and man both work and contribute to retirement, there are differing views about retirement. For a woman, it may be time for them to travel, relax, and spend much deserved, quality time together in their later years. However, for a man, building a fully funded retirement doesn't mean he stops working altogether. It just means he doesn't have to work as much (meaning he has a need to be in the workforce doing something; being productive is his nature).

Aside from their differing views and reasons for retirement, it is expedient for a woman to ask and discuss the road to retirement with her mate. She deserves to have financial peace of mind about retirement just as he does. If he doesn't have an established plan for retirement, why should a woman partner with him for life to share her earned retirement funds? If retirement planning is something he's never seriously given thought to but is willing and committed to working toward, he may be worth consideration as a partner with the condition of receiving professional marital and financial counseling. With divorce and death happening every day, it is no secret that women oftentimes are left holding the bag for taking care of the children, mortgages, living expenses, etc. It is to her benefit to receive appropriate counseling, ensure that beneficiary documents [i.e., retirement accounts, insurances, etc.] are in place early in the marriage, and never give a man sole ownership of joint resources that are being or were built together.

Proverbs 6:6-8 (NLT): *Take a lesson from the ants, you lazybones. Learn from their ways and become wise! Though they have no prince or governor or ruler to make them work, they labor hard all summer, gathering food for the winter.*

NOTE: Bear in mind C.A.T.

7. How many jobs have you had?

Word is, "He can't hold a job for anything in the world."

Straightforward ladies, if he's able-bodied but can't hold a job, he's not worthy of being with you. Too many women overlook telltale signs about his character by not asking simple questions such as this one. Though women are naturally caring motivators and nurturers, in more cases than not, it is hazardously wasteful for any woman to pour her life and resources into a male in hopes of him becoming the man she's envisioning him to be. Sadly and ambitiously, many women figure that investing in an idle man will pay-off for the good of both in the end, producing an abundant life for them. If a man must solely depend on a woman for support because of his laziness, she's become no more than his get rich quick plan which he will exhaust without any regard. The purpose for her asking this question is to eliminate wasting time with someone who's considered unstable, uncommitted, slothful, and misguided. He's not ready for a woman if he's busy neglecting responsibility as a man.

On the other hand, if he's had multiple jobs within reason, there may be a chance that each is a building block toward a goal he is on course for achieving. Case in point, he's in college and has a part-time job during nights and another on weekends, all counting as credit toward his professional career upon graduation; or, he's gaining welding experience by performing and taking various independent jobs to better his skill, which will enhance his chance of gaining full-time employment with a prominent organization. The key is that he's working a plan toward a sustainable goal. Bottom-line, women, use wisdom and caution which will often keep you from being used.

Proverbs 23:4 (NIV): *Do not wear yourself out to get rich; do not trust your own cleverness.*

NOTE: Bear in mind C.A.T.

8. Do you still have any feelings for your ex?

"It doesn't matter, I'm with you."

It does matter and he needs to go. That answer is his way of slyly admitting that he does but he's using the mastered manipulative answer to minimize the woman's concern. A woman neglecting to read between the lines will be highly at risk for a terrible disappointment down the road. However, if he is adamant and his actions are somewhat evident regarding not having feelings for his ex, a woman should proceed in the relationship with caution. Why with caution? Because, sadly, there are men who are great liars but lousy concealers. He may lie to you and tell you exactly what you'd want to hear, but others know because he either talked to his boys and/or has been openly seen with other females at some time and place. If you're not totally convinced that he's over his ex, trust what he's saying but verify his actions – Are there any ongoing links between them? Is he wanting to visit/hang around with his family and friends "just because"? Is he dressing differently, smelling better, or going to the gym a lot? Utilize your keen intuition and investigate like only women can do, in detail! Lastly, go all in if you are confidently sure (without reservation) there are no lingering connections with an ex and he meets criteria for being a husband.

Proverbs 6:27 (NLT): *Can a man scoop a flame into his lap and not have his clothes catch on fire?*

NOTE: Bear in mind C.A.T.

9. Can I see your résumé?

"For what?"

Not many people would consider asking to see a mate's résumé. However, for women to do so would positively be to their advantage. While men may be considered greater liars, women have the counter weapons of intuition and intelligence to investigate the need to know. A man will sell a woman on words of his status and accolades as impressive bait. A wise woman can use this question to confirm whether the goods he is selling are truths or lies. She owes it to herself and her future to know all there is to know about the man she's considering to make a life commitment with. Viewing his employment and education history on said résumé can be used to gather character information. His employment history is a good indicator of commitment and/or of him being goal-oriented, whereas his education provides a background for his level of intelligence. A man can tell a woman whatever he wants to appease her emotionally but it's up to her to probe beyond his words. A good woman warrants truth and reliability from her potential life partner (in marriage).

James 2:18 (NLT): *Now someone may argue, "Some people have faith; others have good deeds." But I say, "How can you show me your faith if you don't have good deeds? I will show you my faith by my good deeds."*

NOTE: Bear in mind C.A.T.

10. Were you born this gender?

"All man, no need to ever question that!"

Not only would it be humiliating but possibly cause long-term psychological effects for a woman to find out after marriage that her husband isn't the biological male she married. Many of her perceived visions of happiness with she and her husband biologically producing children together, hanging with family and friends, etc. have now been completely destroyed. The damage doesn't stop there. The everlasting effect boils over into her spiritual life, if she's a woman of faith and a believer of God's design of male and female. Furthermore, it exposes and makes questionable her identity as a woman not only to herself but family and friends as well. Although it may not be politically correct and acceptable in the secular view of this day and age, it is of the utmost significance that women of faith make it a point to always ask during the dating phase, long before getting too deep in the relationship.

Genesis 5:2 (NIV): *He created them male and female and blessed them. And he named them "Mankind" when they were created.*

NOTE: Bear in mind C.A.T.

11. What would your ex tell me about you?

"Nothing because I'd prefer neither of you talk to the other."

Firstly, if she's his ex and they ended on bad terms, many women may find it more intriguing to speak with the ex. Not a really good idea. There are plenty of witnesses besides the ex who a woman can speak with to corroborate what he has told her (current woman) about them (he and the ex). However, if he and the ex have split on good terms, it may be worthwhile to speak with her. During the conversation, the woman should listen to the totality of shared information (good and bad) and use what is to be addressed further for discussion with him. If the man is as serious about the woman as she is about him, he will make every effort to address her immediate concerns. His focus should be her peace of mind and fortifying their relationship. If the ex provided cautionary information about his character, it is worth next-level discussions with a professional marriage counselor or minister. The woman must stand her ground firmly and not cave into his excuses and apologies over what happened between he and his ex. If he betrayed the trust of his last partner, chances are high for it happening with the current partner – this is why professional counseling should be sought.

Proverbs 12:17 (NLT): *An honest witness tells the truth; a false witness tells lies.*

NOTE: Bear in mind C.A.T.

12. Can I have a talk with your ex?

"That's up to you."

Take it as a word of caution, it may or may not be a good idea. But if he and his ex's relationship ended amicably, there should be no issue speaking with her. Here's the catch. This question is really for an evaluation of his (the man's) manner of answering, not so much for the woman to act on. Does he appear to attempt to divert her from finding out something about him and the ex or possibly other damaging information about himself? Or is he hesitantly being nonchalant in hopes she doesn't talk to his ex? If something is observed or feels shady regarding his responsiveness, the woman may want to do follow-up discreet questionings with his family or friends. If no negative intuitions or indications of something more, chances are he's not hiding anything pertinent. All in all, it is imperative for a woman to exercise wisdom in relationship bonding. Know what you know without a doubt!

Proverbs 24:3 (NIV): *By wisdom a house is built, and through understanding it is established.*

NOTE: Bear in mind C.A.T.

13. What is your credit score?

"Really?!!"

Your answer should be an emphatically resounding, "YES!" There are far too many horror stories of women getting into relationships with men who have terrible credit scores. Once married, those credit scores can and will cost you financially in terms of combined finances and making joint purchases, especially buying a house. The lower the credit score, the higher the interest rates to be paid, which will affect your quality of life in more than one way. Having and maintaining a good credit score (700-749) or a great credit score (750 and above) is ideal and shows one's character, discipline, and integrity. A credit score can be the deciding factor of living in a house, apartment, or on the street. It doesn't necessarily have to be the deal breaker for marriage, but it is worth consideration for the type of future you're planning to have. Though he may be the dream man sent straight from heaven, his credit score can make your life a living hell.

Proverbs 24:27 (NLT): *Do your planning and prepare your fields before building your house.*

NOTE: Bear in mind C.A.T.

14. Have you ever killed someone?

"I'm not telling you!"

If he stares at you or casually laughs it off without ever answering – RUN! Honestly speaking, extreme, uncontrollable anger has driven many people to do unthinkable harms. As a woman, it is of the utmost importance to know and discuss any anger issues or volatile behavior the man has. If he possesses either, you don't want to be the first, next, nor the last person he takes them out on – especially if he has served time in prison for killing or committing violent acts against someone already. This question serves as risk management for your life and is in no way to be taken lightly or humorously. Avoid putting yourself in a compromising position for the sake of having a man – your life, presence, and contribution to society are worth so much more. The time to think selfishly about yourself is knowing who and who not to link up with.

Ecclesiastes 7:9 (NLT): *Control your temper, for anger labels you a fool.*

NOTE: Bear in mind C.A.T.

15. Are you legally married?

"Let's not talk about that, it's difficult to explain."

Advise him that now presents the perfect time for it to be known because you're not about wasting meaningless time. Although all women have intuition, there are those who choose to neglect using it. If a woman's God-given intuitiveness is setting off warning signals, it should not be ignored. Low self-esteem and fear of being alone have been discovered to be the leading two reasons for why women choose to ignore and enter into a relationship with a man who is either married or active with other lovers. If he's not being faithful in his current marriage, what are the chances he'll be with the new woman on the scene? Most importantly for women, is it worth jeopardizing self-worth, a bright future, and who God may be preparing for you?

Sadly, we're living in a day and age where marriages are splitting but never lawfully dissolved. Some couples, though legally married, manage to remain separated for years while living lives as though they're single, with other partners. If there are no official papers on file with the courts that can be produced to show either a legal annulment or divorce, they are still legally married. In such cases, if you're a woman who's dating a man who's married and/or in relationships with other women, stop wasting your time and cut your ties with him immediately. Continuing in a relationship with that man dishonors yourself, his wife, and God.

If he's serious about you, he'll honor your wishes and either make things right with his wife or right by law [i.e., divorce]. In the meantime, stick with God and allow Him to guide you to who He has prepared you for and for you.

Hebrews 13:4 (NLT): *Give honor to marriage, and remain faithful to one another in marriage. God will surely judge people who are immoral and those who commit adultery.*

NOTE: Bear in mind C.A.T.

16. How often do you drink?

"Every now and then."

You should then ask for him to explain that statement more clearly. There's responsible drinking and then there's punch bowl drunkenness. Women, know whether your partner drinks as well as how much/often he does. The subtle effects can easily and quickly become a dependency and fill a home with overwhelming sorrows. Like any central nervous system (CNS) depressant, it slows down brain functioning which creates an inability to react quickly – hence why it is against the law to drink while operating a motorized vehicle. Is drinking alcohol wrong? Certainly NOT! Can a relationship with a man who drinks work out? DEFINTELY! Can a relationship with a man who is a drunkard work out? HIGH RISK OF NOT & POSSIBLY PHYSICAL ABUSE! It's important to understand the consequences of being married to someone who's susceptible to becoming an addict or is an addict and weighing whether it's a risk you're prepared to take.

Like the old liquor commercial says, "Don't let the good taste fool you!"

Isaiah 5:11 (NLV): *It is bad for those who get up early in the morning to run after strong drink! It is bad for those who stay up late in the evening that they may get drunk!*

NOTE: Bear in mind C.A.T.

17. Are you greedy for me?

"What do you mean by 'greedy for you'?"

Your answer should be, "glad you asked!" This question does not pertain to cannibalism, food, or being a glutton. It is an inquiry into the fullness of love that a husband should provide his wife. Translating what is being asked, the question is, "Are you greedy for all of me – heart, body, and mind?" Many women endure pure humiliation brought on by guys who only wanted sexual intimacy, money, food, and/or a roof over their head but never really cared about all aspects of who she is and what she does. It is well known that women crave being loved, appreciated, and respected for the totality of who they are and what they bring to the relationship table. They initially are the ones giving and doing above and beyond, with a nurturing spirit and a heart of love; therefore, many men take for granted their presence and value. This is an upfront question that should be asked, answered, and discussed to the satisfaction of both their understandings prior to marriage. A woman should not lessen her value nor her vision of a husband's standards for any man who's not and unwilling to fairly reciprocate appreciation of heart, body, and mind. When on the same page, it's a wonderful experience to bask in the glory of being appreciatively greedy for one another.

Proverbs 5:15, 18 & 19 (TLB): *Drink from your own well, my son—be faithful and true to your wife. Be happy, yes, rejoice in the wife of your youth. Let her breasts and tender embrace satisfy you. Let her love alone fill you with delight.*

NOTE: Bear in mind C.A.T.

18. Are you a controlling person?

"Not so much controlling, I just like for my expectations to be known and carried out."

Any consideration for a relationship with a guy giving that type of answer should be instantly dissolved. When entering a promising relationship with hopes of marriage, there should be a mutual understanding of both adults being deserving of equal treatment. It is impossible for a relationship to properly thrive if either is exercising a principle of control, submission, fear, and/or obsession. Though being loving, caring, and nurturing are stronger and more natural in a woman than in a man, it would be to her benefit not to give 100% of her emotions, character, and resources to a man who exhibits any inkling of being controlling. Each time she does, she's empowering his behavior and losing her self-identity – making herself more vulnerable for him to control. Finally, beware of men who come across as arrogant, moody, dominant in conversation and actions, inquisitive about your every move, putting his needs first, and wanting to use and maintain control over your finances.

Colossians 3:19 (TLB): *And you husbands must be loving and kind to your wives and not bitter against them nor harsh.*

NOTE: Bear in mind C.A.T.

19. How long do you expect this relationship to last?

"That depends on us."

In other words, he's not looking nor is he ready for anything long-term, like marriage. That makes asking this question crucial for a woman to keep from wasting her time, efforts, and resources, especially if she's seeking something more stable and long-term. If he's unsure or doesn't have any expectations for a long-term relationship [i.e., marriage], don't give him your best days and refrain from being intimate. Moving forward with such a man will only bring many heartaches into your life, not to mention the long-term drama if children are involved.

Additionally, discussing his prospect pertaining to the length of the relationship is advantageous for the woman. It relays to him that she's in focused mode and doesn't have time for play dating. For some women, the biological clock is a prime motivator for commitment from a man whereas for other women, they're ready to get married for a lifetime commitment of making cherished memories, creating a family, and establishing a future with a husband. The best a woman can provide in marriage is what she hasn't provided before marriage. At all costs she must protect her heart, value, and future until a man comes along who's not only worthy of it all but willingly reciprocates the same.

Proverbs 3:27 (NLT): *Do not withhold good from those who deserve it when it's in your power to help them.*

NOTE: Bear in mind C.A.T.

20. Are you emotionally stable?

"I'd like to think so."

That should not suffice as an answer of surety for any woman. Not that a man would honestly admit to being emotionally unstable; however, his physical demeanor can provide a telltale sign or two for either further discussion or investigation through family, friends, and/or an ex. Women should be especially careful and tuned into their intuitive nature when asking this specific question. Read between the lines and dig in with caution if he doesn't provide a direct answer of "yes" or "no", if he provides an evasively non-confident answer of "no", or if he quickly answers and switches to another topic of discussion – exercise C.A.T to the utmost. Pray for God's wisdom and guidance and trust the intuition that He has given you for proceeding or retreating from a relationship with that man. Failure to use prayer, wisdom and intuition has serious consequences that can result in long-term physical, mental, and emotional damage. Be at peace by protecting your peace.

Proverbs 3:5 (NLT): *Trust in the LORD with all your heart; do not depend on your own understanding.*

NOTE: Bear in mind C.A.T.

21. What is your view on extended family members?

"As far as what?"

His response is a typical but serious response a man would give. If the extended family members involve stepchildren, this makes for a great pre-date discussion (see question #30). If the two are already in a serious relationship, this makes for a great pre-marital discussion. Oftentimes, it is the woman who's skeptical about the man's family visiting or temporarily living with she and her husband whereas men, in most cases, are more accommodating to the wife's family visiting or temporarily living with the couple. By nature, women can come across as more possessive while men are more helpful (fixers) by nature. Women like their personal space and control of the home, whereas men prefer having personal time and creative control outside the home. By that concept, when extended family members are thrown into the mix, it is easy to see the ruffled feathers of the woman [i.e., having her personal space disrupted by his family] and the nonchalant attitude of the man (whose personal time and space outside the home isn't being disrupted). Regardless of the differing views and reasons behind them, it is imperative that both discuss and set mutual grounds when it comes to equally welcoming visiting family members on both sides.

1 Timothy 5:8 (TLB): *But anyone who won't care for his own relatives when they need help, especially those living in his own family, has no right to say he is a Christian. Such a person is worse than the heathen.*

NOTE: Bear in mind C.A.T.

22. What are your views on patriarchy/matriarchy?

"Men rule, women follow."

Do not think he will get very far with that answer. First and foremost, it is most important that not only a woman knows her self-worth and place in a relationship (which is as an equal partner) but also that her partner knows, accepts, and respects the totality of who she is and her position within the relationship. With that being said, when asking this question pay very close attention to the man's response. If he believes and/or possess any actions resembling patriarchy (men being supreme to women), it is highly recommended for the woman to end before starting a relationship. However, if the woman strongly thinks there's a chance of him changing his mind and he's open to professional counseling for being educated on relationship equality, there's convincing possibility for the relationship to workout. If he believes and/or possess any actions resembling matriarchy (women being supreme to men), it's a definite bet that he is being manipulative to appease and seize upon her emotions and beliefs while having ulterior motives. It is highly recommended for the woman to end before starting a relationship. Lastly, if he doesn't show any signs of patriarchy or state any false beliefs of supporting matriarchy, it is a good conversation to have and clear the air with an understanding of equality within the relationship.

1 Corinthians 11:3 (TLB): *But there is one matter I want to remind you about: that a wife is responsible to her husband, her husband is responsible to Christ, and Christ is responsible to God.*

NOTE: Bear in mind C.A.T.

23. What are the deal breakers in our relationship?

"You being with another man, period."

Many women would agree that statement is easy for him to say but difficult for many men to keep themselves. When asking this question, it is significantly important to get beyond the generic superficial answer of infidelity. There are way too many people who would say unfaithfulness is a deal breaker but somehow find themselves still in a relationship with the perpetrator. Before marriage, the deal breaker discussion is a must have. Everything needs to be laid on the table and discussed in detail: what are and why those items are deal breakers. A woman's word needs to be taken seriously and respected now before ever entering marriage vows. A woman should not understand this as a mold for herself, for her to be acceptable and adhere to a man's deal breakers, while he continues to do whatever he wants. During the dating phase of a relationship, walking blindly and excusing a man's reckless behavior and lack of devotion for her and the relationship is unacceptable. To eliminate living a life of two wrongs not making a right, a woman should relinquish Mr. Wrong for a godsend Mr. Right!

Proverbs 20:23 (NLT): *The LORD detests double standards; he is not pleased by dishonest scales.*

NOTE: Bear in mind C.A.T.

24. How should we manage our money?

"If we ever merge finances, we'll talk about it then."

In layman terms that response is akin to him saying, "I'm not really too sure about us growing to a level of marriage, let alone willing to have a financial discussion while dating you." Oh, how wrong he is! There's no better time to discuss money management plans than in the present, especially when preparing for the possibility of a future together. Nevertheless, if he's adamant about not discussing financial planning during the dating phase of the relationship, there's a strong possibility that either marriage isn't in his plans (at least not with you) or he's a miser. In marriage it cannot be a "what's mine is mine" type deal for either party. It is crucial that both parties come together in agreement on how finances will be managed prior to marriage.

Marriage calls for having financial discipline and a new realm of responsibilities to include establishing spending priorities. It is always a great idea to have individual spending accounts as well as joint savings (for vacations, gifts, etc.) and checking accounts (for paying bills/living expenses). However, it is essential to have the most important element of trust between both partners for having in place either a will or power of attorney designating one another as beneficiary to the individual spending accounts (in case of emergencies only—i.e., death, etc.). Finally, while dating it is strongly recommended that finances remain separated until there's a legal binding certificate of marriage. In the meantime, protect your financial peace by not giving him your financial piece.

Proverbs 11:24 (NLT): *Give freely and become more wealthy; be stingy and lose everything.*

NOTE: Bear in mind C.A.T.

25. Have you had any financial hardships I need to know about?

"Just a couple of bills that can wait."

Logically, the woman should take that answer as a resounding "YES!" Financial hardships will end a relationship quicker than love started it. There are men who psychologically prey on women and their resources without any regard to their well-being. Oftentimes such men come with a record of financial hardships which they totally disregard and conceal as long as possible. It is extremely unwise for a woman to partner with a man who has known financial hardships or refuses to discuss/disclose those matters. She should consider there being a high probability of him having bad spending habits as well as illiteracy about finances that he's accustomed to and will surely bring into the relationship. Once married, his financial issues become hers and are difficult to cut ties with, costing the woman much more than she may have bargained for.

Proverbs 17:18 (NLT): *It's poor judgment to guarantee another person's debt or put up security for a friend.*

NOTE: Bear in mind C.A.T.

26. Do you find this to be a true statement, "If your car is nasty then so are your home and bodily hygiene?" If so, does it pertain to you?

"Yes, indeed!"

Most often this is an answer a woman should expect to receive from any man. Rarely would a woman find a man having a nasty vehicle. In fact, you will find some men treating their vehicles much better than their partners – true statement! So, why would a woman ask a man this question? The answer is simply to know his take on bodily hygiene and home cleanliness as well as to examine whether it's tolerable or unbearable for her to survive in a relationship. Contrary to popular belief, there are some men who are keen on cleanliness to the point of being either borderline or professionally diagnosed with obsessive compulsive disorder. If you are a woman who does not fit the mold of a man's extreme idea of cleanliness, don't fake like you do because the truth will come to light, and the end result will not be worth the nagging you may have to endure throughout marriage. The same can be said of a woman who is extremely bent on cleanliness. Many would probably agree that neither extreme white-glove cleanliness nor deplorable and pigsty filthiness are attractive attributes. Therefore, what matters most is that normal hygiene routines and home cleanliness are mutually practiced, appreciated, and respected.

Proverbs 21:2 (NLT): *People may be right in their own eyes, but the LORD examines their heart.*

NOTE: Bear in mind C.A.T.

27. Do you believe in God, and what are your thoughts on religion?

"That type of stuff is for suckers!"

This type of statement or belief is one of the main reasons there are more women than men sitting in the pews. When a man is asked this question by a woman [i.e., partner], it is for the intent of her understanding what guides and balances his moral standards and meaning of life. When God isn't a priority, moral standards and accountability are lessened in one's life. It should be a definite matter of importance for a woman of faith (who's open for marriage) to ensure she's linking with a man of like faith. Each having a personal relationship with God is the foundation of a marriage. It's in that relationship with God that both are equipped for making wise, beneficial, and appropriate life decisions. Maintaining those personal relationships with God helps both to grow like-minded as the word of God prosperously governs their marriage, children, and shared life's journey. If the man she's dating doesn't have time for God or so called "religion", she should take heed. If he does believe in God, it will be to her benefit to pray and remain open for God's discernment of that man being the one – He [God] will manifest the answer in some form or another that will bring peace.

Psalm 14:1 (NLT): *Only fools say in their hearts, "There is no God." They are corrupt, and their actions are evil; not one of them does good.*

NOTE: Bear in mind C.A.T.

28. If you could go back in time and change anything, what would you change and why?

"My choice of all things that didn't work out."

Posing this question to a man assists the woman in knowing whether he is living in the past, negatively affected by the past, and/or in need of professional help [i.e., mental treatment] to escape the past. Men being more private than women about devastating situations makes it extremely difficult for them to discuss. Instead of initiating discussion about past regrets, men tend to press forward without ever dealing with/confronting those issues. For one, men assume they'll be judged as being less than a man or weak, so they counter with an overemphasis of accomplishments and show of masculinity. With that in mind, a woman's wisdom is needed in getting to the core of a man with past regrets. It's crucial that he has a level of trust with her that he doesn't have with anyone else. It all starts with her being willing to sit, listen and understand small regrets of his past (without casting judgments) which will lead to him discussing more in-depth, bigger regrets as time proves her trustworthiness. A word of encouragement may be sharing how a start to changing the past is by taking advantage of grace available today. Help him to understand that today (the present) brings a new opportunity to progress beyond what happened yesterday. The past has passed and the only value it can bring to the here and now is knowing it was used to bring both of you where you are today. A woman should let him know how the past was a steppingstone to get him to her.

Philippians 3:13-14 (NLT): *No, dear brothers and sisters, I have not achieved it, but I focus on this one thing: Forgetting the past and looking forward to what lies ahead, I press on to reach the end of the race and receive the heavenly prize for which God, through Christ Jesus, is calling us.*

NOTE: Bear in mind C.A.T.

29. What would I miss out on if I don't choose you as a spouse?

"A man who can love you like only I can."

Although it is a good answer, now is the time for the woman to press for more details. After all, "love" means different things to various people – including being obsessive, abusive, and neglectful. It is very helpful for a woman to realize what sets the man (potential husband) apart from any other man. Yes, she has her own perceptional reasons for being with him, but a woman should not want what she thinks and says about him to be his masqueraded way to her heart. She has the right and deserves to know the real him. This is an opportunity for the man to modestly talk about what he brings to the relationship—make known the value of who he is—and how he views and feels about himself. Golddiggers lower their standards for the security of a man or what he has. Real women look for and marry men who are secure in themselves, complementing the value of who she is. A man whose actions, character, and confidence are above reproach is a man a real woman could appreciate and respect to the utmost.

Proverbs 18:22 (NLT): *The man who finds a wife finds a treasure, and he receives favor from the LORD.*

NOTE: Bear in mind C.A.T.

30. How do you feel about being a stepparent?

"Honestly, I don't know."

This is an undeniably truthful response coming from a man without experience in such a case. For women with children, this is an upfront discussion to have with potential partners. Their children are the most precious possession they have, and caution needs to be taken at all costs when introducing a new man into their lives. More importantly, women should never shy away from having the stepparent discussion with men. There are some men who will be fine with the idea of being a stepparent but once reality sets in [i.e., him having to deal with biological father(s)], it opens up a whole new world of "What did I get myself into?" Unfortunately, there are many biological fathers who do not approve of another man in their children's lives and will cause conflict at every opportunity. Additionally, for the sake of the children, women need to be secure with the potential husband's mindset about being a stepparent. Although the man is preparing to or may have already taken on the responsibility of being a stepparent, he should avoid ever having a distant relationship between them. Lastly, women should observe the man's interactions beyond what he says, have conversations with the children, and most importantly, wisely listen and investigate what their (the children's) concerns are as they relay them to you.

Matthew 13:55 (NLT): *Then they scoffed, "He's just the carpenter's son, and we know Mary, his mother, and his brothers – James, Joseph, Simon, and Judas.*

NOTE: Bear in mind C.A.T.

31. Have you ever been arrested for domestic abuse?

"It was a bum charge on a minor disagreement, nothing big."

Anytime a man seeks to minimize behavior leading to domestic abuse, a woman's intuitive antenna should be maximized. Domestic abuse isn't defined by size but by the operative word "abuse." Whether it's the observance of a man's behavior, his verbally minimizing actions, or what others have witnessed and relayed to a woman, no further evidence is needed to know that he's bad news with uncontrollable anger issues. The hope of him changing is not worth any woman bearing the brunt of "he's getting better" abusive behaviors. Women, beware that love is not exhibited by accepting abuse from a man in any fashion, whether it be verbally, psychologically, or physically. Before getting too deep in a prospective relationship, have eyes and ears wide-open to observe how he reacts when something doesn't go how he believes it should. Listen to his verbal language, beware of his guilt trips, and look for stubbornness. If he lacks patience and understanding, it will be revealed. If the relationship begins with the woman being passive on any inclinations and/or forms of abuse, once married it will only worsen. The best thing a woman can do for an abusive man is depart from him, leaving him in God's hands with a prayer.

Proverbs 22:24-25 (NIV): *Do not make friends with a hot-tempered person, do not associate with one easily angered, or you may learn their ways and get yourself ensnared.*

NOTE: Bear in mind C.A.T.

32. Have you ever attended job corps?

"Are you seriously asking me that?"

A woman's answer should be, "Yes. Is there a problem?" The reasoning behind this question about job corps is to solicit honesty, awareness, and gather hidden background information about a man she is considering being in a relationship with. Yes, the question does come off kind of weird for a guy who hasn't been to job corps, but it's an intriguing question for the guy who has been to job corps. He may have his reason(s) for not revealing it to the woman sooner; however, by her asking this question, it lessens reservations and any shame he may have as well as allows for him to positively connect with the woman emotionally, with a willingness to discuss the intricacies of his ups and downs, known and unknown. This discussion adds weight to the woman's discernment on whether a man is sincerely ready for a committed relationship. Besides, she can play a tremendous role of inspiration for his continual progress.

Philippians 3:15-16 (NLT): *But we must hold on to the progress we have already made.*

NOTE: Bear in mind C.A.T.

33. What is your highest level of education?

"Completed high school and have a couple years of college in."

Not a bad answer but still warrants further explanation as to whether he is still attending college or has given up. For some women, a man's education doesn't matter as much as him having a persona of toughness. However, please know that education is fundamental. In any relationship, there's much to be learned about the other person that can be taken way off course if there's no standard of education and/or common-sense between the two. Oftentimes (not all the time) many who drop out of school do so with a mindset of believing they know more than what can be taught in school and/or by anyone. However, they fail to grasp the bigger picture and fundamentals of life. The most powerful tool humans have is a brain. When the brain isn't exercised and strengthened to handle the teachable mental toughness of acceptable and positive progressive norms of society, it will quickly and easily feed on false perceptions and an untamed "do or die" mentality leading to further ignorance. A woman linking with a man who's apathetically comfortable sets herself up for carrying a load she isn't meant to carry alone. Sure, with love one can work through anything, but without some form of education and common-sense a relationship will be limited in what can be handled.

Proverbs 24:10 (NLV): *If you are weak in the day of trouble, your strength is small.*

NOTE: Bear in mind C.A.T.

34. Is marriage or monogamy something you truly want?

"I'll go with whatever you're down for."

Okay, that man can quickly be scratched off the potential list. Women, guess what? Men need clarity, which is why this question needs to be asked sooner rather than later in a relationship. There needs to be a mutual understanding of what each is seeking short- and long-term. A woman needs to KNOW that she's the 'one and only' in a man's life and not be so quick to THINK she's the only one. Most women view dating as being on the road to marriage. On the opposite spectrum, most men see dating as a means to gain sexual experiences, bragging rights, and fulfill deceptional definitions of manhood. For a woman to keep herself from being in the fold of a man's "harem", she must stand her ground based on the uncompromisable standards of her faith and morals. If in a "serious" relationship but the man says, fears, or believes he can't commit to just that one woman, women should avoid deceiving themselves by fictitiously hearing, believing otherwise, and compromising their standards for the sake of keeping him. Especially for the women who are wanting to bring precious children in this world, think and pray for God's strength to preserve you for the man He has prepared or is preparing for you.

1 Corinthians 7:2 (NLT): *But because there is so much sexual immorality, each man should have his own wife, and each woman should have her own husband.*

NOTE: Bear in mind C.A.T.

35. Are you willing to collaborate on decision-making if we both bring in a fruitful salary?

"I'll have to wait and see because I will be the man of my house."

That would be an unintelligent answer for any man to give. This question offers a woman insight into if and how a man centers decision-making on sexism and/or salary. In a relationship [i.e., marriage], decision-making is a partnership discussion in which both parties voice their reasons, hear one another out completely, and agree upon the result that best benefits all. Salary should not be the deciding factor on whether one or the other has say-so or not. There is no difference or superiority with the one who is working a job outside the home and the other who is maintaining the home. However, if there is a strong disagreement on a matter, both should seek the wisdom of God in prayer and scripture together and individually, then come together again to discuss the matter further. If a woman is interested in a man who is headstrong and bent on basing decision-making on sexism and/or salary, it would be wise for both to seek professional counseling (preferably godly counsel).

1 Peter 3:7 (NLT): *In the same way, you husbands must give honor to your wives. Treat your wife with understanding as you live together. She may be weaker than you are, but she is your equal partner in God's gift of new life. Treat her as you should so your prayers will not be hindered.*

NOTE: Bear in mind C.A.T.

36. Are you willing to assist in daily household chores?

"That's your job!"

Stop the presses! No, he did not just say that! Sadly, that is an expected response from a sexist man who is or may have been misguidedly trained to think such a way about a woman. Does this make him ineligible as marriage material? Being in that current state of mind does; however, if there's a strong probability of him being open-minded for change, further discussion, and counseling, there's a chance for a relationship to go forward. But if he is a headstrong sexist who feels he's correct and has no need for change, furthering a relationship is based on the woman's willingness or unwillingness to do so. The woman should consider how messy this guy may and/or can be and yet would expect her to clean up behind him. Is it really a predicament she's able to accept for life? A woman should never short-change herself for the sake of having a man who's cheating her to establish his own self-worth.

Philippians 2:3 (NLV): *Nothing should be done because of pride or thinking about yourself. Think of other people as more important than yourself.*

NOTE: Bear in mind C.A.T.

37. What are your expectations as a father/husband?

"To be the best of both."

The idea behind asking this question is for a woman to not only solicit a man's perception of being a husband and father, but for her to compare it alongside her own perception. Their differences open the door for discussion in attaining an acceptable balance. By her knowing his perceptions and his not being passive, it also tells whether he's given forethought to being a husband and father. If he has given forethought and presents a compelling case, he just may well be worth her interest and time. His sincerity helps bring a sense of security for her about being in the relationship and potentially for being a wife and mother. A positive answer from the man also shows his willingness to be held equally accountable and responsible as a partner and parent. It's essential for a woman to know without a doubt that her partner is not only up to the task of marriage and fatherhood but also fully prepared and committed to her and to their children. Trust is the key element that empowers a couple's giving, living, and doing their best for the family!

Psalm 127:3 & 5 (TLB): *Children are a gift from God; they are his reward. Happy is the man who has his quiver full of them.*
Matthew 19:4-6 (TLB): *"Don't you read Scriptures?" he replied. "In them it is written that at the beginning God created man and woman, and that a man should leave his father and mother, and be forever united to his wife. The two shall become one—no longer two, but one! And no man may divorce what God has joined together."*

NOTE: Bear in mind C.A.T.

38. Who comes first and why – spouse or children?

"Happy wife, happy life."

This is a sensitive topic, primarily because actions speak louder than words and maturity needed among both parties. Mature men understand, accept, and appreciate a wife's love, care, and protection of their child(ren). He has bought into the concept of partnership in marriage and need not to ever question his place in his wife's life. There is serious doubt that most women would seek a man-child for a husband. He can't go through life behaving as a child himself and competing for those same affections from her that are reserved for their children. That is while the child is a child. However, when that child has become a young adult (graduates 12th grade and/or college), it's time for the wife to cut the strings and allow that grown individual (especially males) to take flight. Rarely would a man enable the immaturity of an adult offspring by allowing the individual to idly lounge around their [husband/wife] house without a job, having any responsibilities and/or providing contributions.

From a logical standpoint, the man realizes it's not doing that adult son/daughter (especially son) any good and will only lead to friction between he and his wife. With many woman having a heart of compassion (expressly for their children), they typically go out of the way for their adult offspring, treating them as though they're still little children. By doing so, the man and woman are no longer operating as one because she has now prioritized another adult above her husband which creates unneeded but warranted tension within the marriage.

Ephesians 5:21 (LB): *Honor Christ by submitting to each other.*
Ephesians 5:33 (NLT): *So again I say, each man must love his wife as he loves himself, and the wife must respect her husband.*
Ephesians 6:1 (LB): *Children, obey your parents; this is the right thing to do because God has placed them in authority over you.*

NOTE: Bear in mind C.A.T.

39. What are you passionate about?

"Working."

That may be a true answer but it's not an absolute answer. It doesn't necessarily indicate he doesn't or wouldn't have time for a relationship. It may be his way of saying his passion for working is tied into his preparedness for a mate. His vision of being in a relationship is one that is based on affordability and balance of time, efforts, and resources. This would be a man who doesn't want to burn the candle at both ends with a result of nothingness. He chooses to be equipped and stable (financially, mentally, and professionally) for a mate rather than enduring the extra stresses of dating and spending (time and resources) for her happiness all the while hurting his focus of a secure future. Conversely, there are men who truly are over-passionate about work due to worry about the future, which deters their attention from a relationship. This could and oftentimes does cause serious issues within a relationship. If there is a strong connection between the woman and the man, it would befit both to discuss and come to an understanding of either continuing in the relationship or moving on separately – maybe there's a chance to reconnect later or just maybe there's a true soulmate who God has prepared and has waiting in the wings.

Proverbs 22:29 (MSG): *Observe people who are good at their work—skilled workers are always in demand and admired; they don't take a backseat to anyone.*

NOTE: Bear in mind C.A.T.

40. What are your short- and long-term goals, and what are you actively doing to achieve them?

"To just have a better life."

His answer will require further discussion and details, such as defining a "better life" and who's included in it. It is the preference of many women to link with a mate who not only has goals but is working toward realizing them. If a woman is satisfied to settle with an idle mate, it may illustrate a low self-esteem. As the saying goes, "A person can do bad all by him or herself." It is not ideal for any woman to take on the dead weight and responsibilities of a lazy man. It's imperative for a woman to observe a man working toward having a prosperous and healthy future with and for the two of them rather than her fantasizing about him having potential and wishing he would do something rather than nothing.

Knowing a man's short- and long-term goal(s) respectfully presents her the opportunity to support and/or decide on whether it is the road she can see herself being a part of for life. For example, some women may love the idea of being married to a military man but can't deal with the extended separation periods of deployments and vice versa for men. For reasons such as that, discussing short- and long-term goals should also encompass the struggles to be endured by both parties, not just the ups or how smoothly things are presently going. A man's sincerity about goals is evident in what he's doing now – women take note.

Proverbs 20:13 (NIV): *Do not love sleep or you will grow poor; stay awake and you will have food to spare.*

NOTE: Bear in mind C.A.T.

41. Were you ever abused?

"With all due respect, that's none of your business."

Quite the contrary, being in a serious relationship or married, makes it the woman's business to know. Though he may not want to talk about it, if he's serious about the relationship and marrying the woman, in due time after having established trust with the woman, he will soon talk. However, the woman must exercise extreme patience since abuse is not something men are necessarily comfortable talking about with anyone. This is partly because he mentally processes it as an embarrassment and may feel he would be viewed as less than a man. However, it is important for this discussion to take place primarily so that the woman can provide support and be aware of the safe and danger zones regarding what triggers his emotions.

A woman having knowledge of a man's past abuse is not ever to be used as a weapon against him. It is for her to provide assurance of love, support, and/or recommend/join in for professional counseling. Furthermore, it aids her in helping him maintain self-control rather than engaging in unexplainable and damaging outbursts of wrath. If there ever arises an issue of the man directing harm or bodily injury toward the woman, she has no choice but to depart for her own safety. No woman should ever think or believe that she alone can change a man from being abusive nor feel that she's helping him by accepting his abuse. A woman who's willing to love beyond and walk with a man through a troubling past is a godsend if he's not reflecting harm or injury on/toward her.

Proverbs 14:29 (NLT): *People with understanding control their anger; a hot temper shows great foolishness.*

NOTE: Bear in mind C.A.T.

42. Would you consider seeing a mental health professional, if advised or needed?

"For what? There's nothing wrong with me."

That answer proves the validity of this question and why this discussion is a must have. Many men are prone to believing they have it all together and that only a weak man needs to seek the help of a mental health professional. Truth be told, that very erroneous thinking is why men bottle up destructive emotions and stressors which become a detriment to their health and affects their relationship with those around them. The benefit of a woman asking this question is to know how the man views mental health and to seize the opportunity to educate him on the importance of seeking a professional; this can help one maintain mental health and stability for the sake of family and, more importantly, living a peaceful life with a mind discharged of less 'stinking thinking'. Although men may feel secure in their beliefs and behaviors of toughness, with the help of a loving woman, there's a strong probability of them becoming susceptible to having a change of mind.

Romans 12:2 (NLT): *Don't copy the behavior and customs of this world, but let God transform you into a new person by changing the way you think. Then you will learn to know God's will for you, which is good and pleasing and perfect.*

NOTE: Bear in mind C.A.T.

43. Are you saving for retirement?

"Reaching retirement age isn't a guarantee so I live for today."

Sadly, that response is a reality for many men across the nation, which is also the main reason those same men don't or will not have a healthy retirement life to enjoy. A man saving for retirement serves a woman's interest for peace of mind during the latter years to come. She shouldn't carelessly position herself in a predicament of mere survival due to her and/or her mate's poor planning. Someone in the marriage must be willing to give thought for and be proactive about financial planning for retirement. The discussion of saving for retirement should occur during the early dating phase of a relationship. It is of the utmost importance that time and health are capitalized on. Not working equals no contributions toward retirement, which results in survival struggles. The healthiest years for working are the years of one's youth – it is the season to maximize on earnings, savings, and investments. Although no one is promised tomorrow it doesn't negate planning for it. If a man isn't mindfully willing to make the financial transition by thinking of his wife's stability (if something were to happen to him), it would be prudent for her to strongly reconsider if he's what she's looking for in a commitment of marriage.

Proverbs 12:15 (LB): *A fool thinks he needs no advice, but a wise man listens to others.*

NOTE: Bear in mind C.A.T.

44. Do you communicate (i.e., text, talk, meet for lunch, etc.) on a regular basis with people you are attracted to?

"If I was, I would be a fool to admit it to you."

There's nothing abnormal about being attracted to someone by way of admiration. Where the problem arises is when that admiration is illustrated through explicit thoughts and action [i.e., flirtations, secret message exchanges, alone times, etc.]. Such actions should be more than reason for concern in the heart of the man as well as his partner (when revealed). However, a man's pride, guilt, and embarrassment will prevent him from admitting to his partner that he's been communicating with someone he's attracted to on a regular basis. What he needs to understand is that his being honest with his partner for the sake of their relationship should be more important than his apprehensions about her response. A woman posing this question is, quite frankly, giving the man a courtesy way out by opening the door for a mature adult discussion. During the discussion, as she presents her take on the matter, it would strongly benefit him to listen and make mental notes of how she feels about the situation. Out of respect for her feelings and the relationship, it would be wise for him to put forth every effort to empathize and make the necessary adjustments that would keep peace in the relationship. That special woman is seeking a man who will give her his undivided attention and who is ready to live a new life solely committed to her, as she is to him. She has no patience or time to waste on or wonder about shadiness.

2 Corinthians 5:17 (NLT): *This means that anyone who belongs to Christ has become a new person. The old life is gone; a new life has begun!*

NOTE: Bear in mind C.A.T.

45. Are you still intimately involved with your ex?

"Do you really want to know?"

As soon as he says that, run! This is definitely a need-to-ask pre-date question. All too often, lives are lost, and relationships are destroyed because of deceptive statements of supposed ex-partners being out of the picture. Women possess the most acute intuitiveness and know within their hearts whether something is awry about their mates. When those convincing signals are going off, stop fighting against the grain in false hope. Sever the ties with that man and increase your time with God so that He may bring to you just who He has prepared for you – and you for him. Conversely, if the man's ex is truly out of the picture and he's sincere about being in a relationship with the new woman, that woman needs to know without a doubt that it is just she and him. Women should keep their hearts guarded and beware of getting involved with a man who hasn't severed intimacy ties with his ex – the results will only produce devastating consequences throughout the new relationship, with the new woman suffering the most.

Colossians 3:5 (NIV): *"Put to death, therefore, whatever belongs to your earthly nature: sexual immorality, impurity, lust, evil desires and greed, which is idolatry."*

NOTE: Bear in mind C.A.T.

46. What major trauma(s) have you experienced and are still dealing with?

"Oh, I'm good to go now."

"Now" is the operative word, suggesting there was such an experience. This question is in no way intended for casting judgment. Rather, it is for awareness and discussion of how a woman (partner) can assist and/or further understand the man (husband to be) through knowledge of any traumatic incident he may have experienced or is currently experiencing. His candidness through discussion presents a form of intimate bonding with the woman. Intimacy within a relationship certainly doesn't start and end with sex. It is a shared culmination of experiences – past, present, future, good and bad, rights and wrongs, failures and successes, etc. – it's getting to know, accepting what is known, and loving and supporting in spite of. Frankly, it is love put forth through knowing, accepting, loving, and supporting your partner to a degree greater than anyone else can, has, or will. It's providing support whether needed or not. Most importantly, it's praying for one another and realizing both parties are answers God has delivered into each other life. A wife's heart is demonstrated by doing all she can to make life comfortable and pleasing for her husband. Her devoted care for him is God's blessing in action.

1 Peter 5:7 (NLT): *Give all your worries and cares to God, for he cares about you.*

NOTE: Bear in mind C.A.T.

47. What's your stance on forgiveness?

"It's dependent on the degree of the issue."

That's an honest answer across the board due to many not fully understanding the need for and power of forgiveness, thus making this a great question for a woman to ask a man. It's no hidden fact that men do and say things that women are more apt to forgive than men when the shoes are on the other feet. It is the nature of women to have hearts of compassion which complement the pairing with men. It's not so much that men don't have or are incapable of showing compassion, it's just not a center of their focus. Men are more attuned to pressing through an issue rather than dealing with the root cause(s). By doing so, their comprehension of compassion and forgiveness becomes a bit skewed with them temporarily ignoring the problem and refocusing attention on what they feel is more important.

A woman asking this question is not doing so because she's planning to do something that would require his forgiveness and wanting to know the consequences upfront. This question is mainly meant to discuss any outstanding issues in his life that need to be addressed. It's a terrible situation for a woman to find herself dating or married to a man who is continually stuck in the past about how another woman (or other women) have cheated, lied, stole, etc. It makes it extremely difficult to grow together in a relationship when he is constantly questioning and comparing everything the current woman does based on what was done to him in the past. He may be a great man in many ways but harboring unforgiveness is something hard to contend with. Before a woman moves forward with this type of man, it is strongly advised that both get wise and professional counseling. Without counseling, the woman will find herself either passing on what could've been an incredible man or marrying a most untrusting, bitter man which in turn may lead to an untrusting, bitter marriage – full of regrets.

Ephesians 4:31-32 (NLT): *Get rid of all bitterness, rage, anger, harsh words, and slander, as well as all types of evil behavior.*

Instead, be kind to each other, tenderhearted, forgiving one another, just as God through Christ has forgiven you.

NOTE: Bear in mind C.A.T.

48. How often are you willing to have sex?

"Are you ready now?"

That's the answer for the average youthful stud but not so much as aging becomes a factor. Sex is something that too many relationships are heavily focused and built on. It's become the leading motivator that steers people toward marriage, adultery, fornication, and broken marriages. Sadly, it is the power that many respect and worship all the while neglecting moral standards, faith, vows, and commitment. A woman asking a man this question should be readily prepared for him to give an answer based on the present without giving any thought about future stamina, health issues, or consideration of her input. He wants to appear as Superman in every sense and will not dare belittle his machismo by speaking truth about his sexual prowess.

Onward, without a doubt, sex does play a major role in marriage hence why it needs to and should be discussed in-depth between the man and woman. There should be a mutual respect and understanding regarding the need as well as the timing and/or amount of sex within marriage. On average, as men get older there comes a decrease in sexual stamina whereas women experience an increased appetite – in the golden age years, it usually all balances out for both. In either case, both sex drives should be reasonably accommodated by each party as much as possible. Lastly, let not sex serve as the foundation of the marriage in place of unconditional love. For sure, it will take love to get through everything when sex fails.

1 Corinthians 7:5 (NIV): *Do not deprive each other except perhaps by mutual consent and for a time, so that you may devote yourselves to prayer. Then come together again so that Satan will not tempt you because of your lack of self-control.*

NOTE: Bear in mind C.A.T.

49. When was your last relationship and why did it end?

"It's been a while. See I've been just dating here and there, no real relationship."

Right off the bat, intuitive antennas should be up and detecting "not ready." Anyway, this should be one of the top five upfront questions to ask a man of interest during the pre-dating phase. Knowing when and the reason behind his last relationship ending provides insight into his extent of commitment to a relationship as well as what may have been his part in the relationship ending. If he's behaving shiftily in discussing the question, that's a red flag. If he's being open and forthright, that's commendable. Commendable can lead a woman into tolerating a man's sob story, but the fact is that it doesn't mean he has bettered himself and/or is ready for her. Unfortunately, there are preying men who are great at playing on women's emotions of pity just to get what they can from her. Warning to the women: beware and dig deep in discussion about this topic. It is imperative for women to ask, discuss in-depth, and ensure he's ready for what she's prepared to sacrifice [i.e., emotions, time, efforts, and resources] for the sake of a relationship leading to marriage and without having to deal with residue from past relationships.

Proverbs 25:19 (NLT): *Putting confidence in an unreliable person in times of trouble is like chewing with a broken tooth or walking on a lame foot.*

NOTE: Bear in mind C.A.T.

50. How do you react in tense situations?

"Voice my opinion, give those involved a warning, and leave it at that."

Nothing worse than a hot-headed person making a mountain out of a molehill. Listening is the key to decelerating a tense situation. It is very difficult to achieve common ground in making progress if both are simultaneously talking over one another. Cooler heads can only prevail when one is mature enough to and exercises the power of listening. Women should not expect men to emotionally respond as they do just as men should not expect women to physically respond as they do. When tense situations arise, it's time for both parties to take a breather, discuss the origin, and develop an agreeable plan of action for correction. There is no need to blow things completely out of proportion to the point of causing a lifetime relationship to be on the brink of destruction in a moment. This question is another definite pre-date question – no need of having to find out the hard way.

James 1:19 (NLT): *Understand this, my dear brothers and sisters: You must all be quick to listen, slow to speak, and slow to get angry.*

NOTE: Bear in mind C.A.T.

51. What's your take on current matters in the world?

"It is what it is. My concern is what's going on in my own world."

While it's good to know he's concerned about what's going on in his own world, that's a limited focus. Being abreast of current matters of the world is critical for understanding how the bigger picture of things going on outside has trickling effects on our individual lives and future plans. The ability to live a fruitful life involves being in the know about current matters of the world, not being consumed in fear or living trapped in a bubble. Many opportunities are missed due to lack of knowledge regarding current matters.

 Oppositely and interestingly, there are many couples who have split because of disagreements about what each support [i.e., politics, sports, ideas, etc.]. In the dating phase of a relationship, if there's something that either the man or woman simply can't and won't compromise on, they have a choice of either staying clear of that particular topic by agreeing to disagree or they can relieve themselves from the relationship. It would be most advantageous for both parties to discuss and iron out the differences then rather than making later attempts in marriage. Word of caution – it would be wise for neither partner to take extreme interest in current world matters to the point of allowing it to destroy their marriage or transforming him or her into someone who represents something far different from their Christian faith.

1 Peter 5:8 (NIV): *Be alert and of sober mind. Your enemy the devil prowls around like a roaring lion looking for someone to devour.*

NOTE: Bear in mind C.A.T.

Questions From Women
That Men Do Not Answer

Questions From Women
That Men Do Not Answer

1. Do you think she's pretty?

Plain and simple, many men do not answer this question because they want to keep the peace by not engaging in a trivial conversation concerning their thoughts about another woman. A man's stance is that he's with the woman he wants and that's all that matters. Furthermore and unfortunately, many men give into the stereotypical belief that if it's their (women's) "time of the month" when asking this question to not answer because of their (women's) supposed overreaction. Thoughts come and go but what matters most and above all else is the reality of who is in his life. Besides, in a seasoned relationship [i.e., marriage], that's built on trust and honesty, the wife should already know his discernment of beauty.

1 Peter 3:3-4 (NLT): *Don't be concerned about the outward beauty of fancy hairstyles, expensive jewelry, or beautiful clothes. You should clothe yourselves instead with the beauty that comes from within, the unfading beauty.*

2. How do you feel?

Posing this question to some men comes across as a requirement for them to be sensitive – an untapped emotion they view as weak for a man. Many men choose to ignore discussing their feelings to ease the stresses in their lives rather than getting into a prolonged conversation with their caring partner which they consider 'letting down the man-guard,' and it being foreign for many to do. There's also that fear of not being able to properly articulate their feelings, which will anger many men because of false presumptions that the woman would not be able to relate or grasp what he's trying to say – it may be true, or it may not be true, depending on the maturity of their mate. Getting a man to lower his guard will require time, trust, and a caring attitude.

Proverbs 13:3 (NLT): *Those who control their tongue will have a long life, opening your mouth can ruin everything.*

3. Would you sleep with her?

Jokingly, he may already have (just kidding). Many men view this as a setup question – a setup for an argument the man isn't prepared for because he's incapable of thinking fast enough to answer the onslaught of subsequent questions the woman is going to bring. Therefore, they will not answer, no matter how adamant the women are about "needing" them to answer. The general belief among men is that answering this question is a death sentence to all intimacy with their mate for a long while which will only magnify many insignificant issues, disturbing all peace in the home. Now if the woman has to question whether the man did or did not sleep with "her", there's no need of her asking what she already knows.

Matthew 5:28 (NLT): *But I say, anyone who even looks at a woman with lust has already committed adultery with her in his heart.*

4. Do you think my sister is hot?

Generally, this will not be answered by a man because of his respect for his mate and to avoid further discussion [i.e., an argument]. A man knows that if he truthfully answers this question as a "yes", he will never be trusted to be around his wife's sister for any reason during any event (including family reunions). Additionally, he will be convinced that his mate doesn't care if his response was innocent and without any preconceived notions of being attracted to her sister, it will be forever engrained as a nagging thought of him and her sister seizing an opportunity to act on. Also, let's not forget mentioning the labels and snide remarks he'll have to endure hearing under her breath. Therefore, he refuses to partake in this subject matter conversation with his mate for the sake of both their sanity.

Colossians 3:5 (TLB): *Away then with sinful, earthly things; deaden the evil desires lurking within you; have nothing to do with sexual sin, impurity, lust, and shameful desires; don't worship the good things of life, for that is idolatry.*

5. If I was disabled, would you still love me?

Men who are honestly unsure will not answer this question to keep from hurting the woman's feelings and/or being viewed in a negative light by her if he were to answer "no." Many men commonly prefer seeing their wife's beauty and attraction just as they did when they first met or as they are currently. They can't fathom the thought of their wives being disabled and frankly are very uncomfortable even discussing such a possibility. Is there something wrong with having a disabled spouse? Certainly not! However, it is something many men can't and don't imagine her as being, choosing rather to avoid having their love judged by a disability. The mere thought presents a psychological fray that a man is simply unwilling to contend with. Does and will he continue to love her in heart? In most cases the answer is "yes." Most men aren't good emotional grapplers and will require further counseling about love.

Ephesians 5:25 (NLV): *Husbands, love your wives. You must love them as Christ loved the church. He gave His life for it.*

6. If you were a woman, who would be your dream husband?

This is a question that will have many men feeling very uncomfortable. The idea of a man seeing himself as a woman and having a dream husband will not be entertained because it goes against the grain of him knowing who he is, and that's the bottom-line. In no way is he illustrating homophobic fears or passing judgment, he just unapologetically and proudly accepts his design and birth as a male – no ifs, ands, or buts about it – especially if he's a man of faith.

Romans 1:26-28 (NIV): *Because of this, God gave them over to shameful lusts. Even their women exchanged natural sexual relations for unnatural ones. In the same way the men also abandoned natural relations with women and were inflamed with lust for one another. Men committed shameful acts with other men, and received in themselves the due penalty for their error. Furthermore, just as they did not think it worthwhile to retain the knowledge of God, so God gave them over to a depraved mind, so that they do what ought not to be done.*

7. Who's your "man-crush"?

Firstly, he views this question as inappropriate for a partner/wife to ask. Secondly, he'd probably wonder why his partner/wife is asking this question as though she has noticed something about him (conflicting with his masculinity) that he's unaware of, which poses another issue that needs to be addressed. Lastly, he may consider her asking this question as being disrespectful to his manliness as well as their relationship and faith. Therefore, he may resolve to not answer nor entertain this question.

Proverbs 4:24 (NLT): *Avoid all perverse talk; stay away from corrupt speech.*

8. Do you think he's handsome?

Some more secure men may answer this question with no problem. However, for many men, how another man looks is not in their thoughts for judgment, especially in determining level of handsomeness. They will not waste their brain cells considering how handsome another man may or may not look. For them, this is a question women should be having with their girlfriends. A man who doesn't answer this question is a man who's offended by it. He's probably thinking, "Why is she not talking to me about how handsome I look?" He honestly could not care less how handsome another man appears to be.

Proverbs 4:24 (NLT): *Avoid all perverse talk; stay away from corrupt speech.*

9. Can we talk about a personal past trial in your life?

This is a question normally not answered by a man who has witnessed a loved one experience or been personally involved in a traumatic ordeal himself. Though there are or could be multiple reasons why he chooses not to answer, the most probable is that of trust followed closely by embarrassment. Many men who have either witnessed or endured trauma tend to think of themselves as victims which is a "no-no" depending on the cultural environment and leads to them suppressing the issue, even though counseling may be needed. Furthermore, he may be unwilling to discuss the issue with a partner or wife due to how well he knows her character (i.e., gossiper, may use the information as a weapon during arguments, etc.) – all it takes is one argument for him to observe how far she'll go to hurt his ego, which may not turn out too good for either of them.

Micah 7:5 (NLV): *Do not trust a neighbor. Do not put trust in a friend. Be careful what you say even with her who lies in your arms.*

10. How many intimate partners have you had?

This an unwavering "DO NOT ANSWER" with the truth question for men. Most of those who choose to answer will provide a smaller than actual number. For those who do not answer, it's for the sake of the current relationship. He has high respect for the woman he's currently with and considers it unfruitful information for growing their relationship. As far as he's concerned, regrets of the past should be left in the past; he's willing and ready to start afresh with the woman before him now. Forcing a man to answer by dwelling on a question such as this may recreate a spark within him for the "fun" of the past which will be to the woman's disadvantage.

Proverbs 29:20 (NIV): *Do you see someone who speaks in haste? There is more hope for a fool than for them.*

11. Are you promiscuous?

This is a simple question that any man who's in a serious relationship should have no problem answering. However, for those who refuse to answer, it should serve as a caution for women. It is highly likely that a man's refusal to answer is because the truth is "yes", and he doesn't want it to impact his current relationship. Ironically, it will and does impact his current relationship because it casts doubt in the woman's mind. Here's a word of wisdom for women who are dating questionable men: if you've been hearing rumors of him being promiscuous and your intuition radar is going off the charts, take heed and beat feet.

2 Timothy 2:22 (NLV): *Turn away from the sinful things young people want to do. Go after what is right. Have a desire for faith and love and peace. Do this with those who pray to God from a clean heart.*

Romans 13:13 (NLT): *Because we belong to the day, we must live decent lives for all to see. Don't participate in the darkness of wild parties and drunkenness, or in sexual promiscuity and immoral living, or in quarreling and jealousy.*

12. Do you possess toxic masculinity?

Men who do not answer this question are either insulted by it or on the defense about it. For most who view it as offensive, it is because their character is being questioned when there's clear evidence to support otherwise. For many who become defensive, they're indiscreetly proving the existence of that toxic masculinity. The defensiveness can be in the form of downplaying the issue, displaying an arrogant behavior, deflecting the question, etc. A woman should be persistent for an answer, regardless how the man feels about it. If he's insistent on not verbally answering, friendship may be the only option until further discussion takes place.

Domineering – 1 Peter 5:3 (NLT): *Don't lord it over the people assigned to your care, but lead them by your own good example.*
Selfishness – Philippians 2:3 (NLT): *Don't be selfish; don't try to impress others. Be humble, thinking of others as better than yourselves.*
Arrogance – Roman 12:3 (NIV): *For by the grace given me I say to every one of you: Do not think of yourself more highly than you ought, but rather think of yourself with sober judgment, in accordance with the faith God has distributed to each of you.*

13. What are your fears?

Men who do not answer this question may have had bad past experiences of women using their revealed fears as tools against them, hence giving them reason for being silent on the matter. Also, there are men who feel that disclosing fears makes questionable their masculinity because they've sincerely bought into the antiquated notion that "real men" fear nothing. This is not anything that a woman should be alarmed about. In the passing of time, growing together, and gaining of trust, there's a strong possibility that he will arrive at the point of having candid conversations about the subject matter.

2 Timothy 1:7 (NLV): *For God did not give us a spirit of fear. He gave us a spirit of power and of love and of a good mind.*

14. Are you self-aware?

The refusal to answer this question should not be taken personally. Many men are satisfied operating within a black and white world, giving no consideration to gray areas – answers they comprehend are straightforward yes or no, is or is not, right or wrong, etc., with a "go with the flow" mentality, disregarding their personal feelings and character. They prefer taking what they consider to be the easiest and quickest route that produces desired results, although and oftentimes there may be better methods of achieving better results. Therefore, men who refuse to answer the question consider it an insult to their intelligence because they assume they know better for themselves. Another possibility is that they may be afraid of showing their ignorance about what being self-aware really means, resulting in them being comfortably unaware.

Galatians 6:4 (NLV): *Everyone should look at himself and see how he does his own work. Then he can be happy in what he has done. He should not compare himself with his neighbor.*

15. Are you able to be transparent and vulnerable?

Should be an easy enough question any man would be willing and ready to provide an answer to. However, there are some men who will not. Hearing words like 'transparent' and 'vulnerable' come off as a show of weakness based on the cultural environment the man comes from. Instead of admitting and discussing their flaws and/or struggles, they default to suppression – never dealing with underlying issues and forever wondering what is driving their attitudes of distrust, animosity, aloofness, etc. This can be overcome by the woman praying for him, slowly educating him (verbally and by example), not being judgmental in conversations, and being patient, allowing time to take its course.

James 5:16 (TLB): *Admit your faults to one another and pray for each other so that you may be healed. The earnest prayer of a righteous man has great power and wonderful results.*

16. What is your parenting style?

Not answering this question is a strong indication that either the man isn't interested in being a parent, doesn't know how to be a parent (due to lack of parenting in his own upbringing), or he believes in parenting on a whim (addressing what needs to be addressed once the child(ren) arrives). For either reason, his refusal to answer or discuss this isn't acceptable for a woman who envisions having a family someday with him. The woman should stand firm in her desire and pursuit of having a family; however, it is strongly recommended they both seek professional pre-marital counseling before furthering their relationship. In marriage, producing and parenting children requires both to be on the same page.

2 Corinthians 12:14 (NLT): *Now I am coming to you for the third time, and I will not be a burden to you. I don't want what you have—I want you. After all, children don't provide for their parents. Rather, parents provide for their children.*
Proverbs 4:3-4 (NLT): *For I, too, was once my father's son, tenderly loved as my mother's only child. My father taught me, "Take my words to heart. Follow my commands, and you will live…"*

17. Do you love your mother more than me?

This is a question that some men will have a surprised or ambivalent facial expression in response to. It's the look that says, "I can't believe you, as an adult, are asking me such a childish question." Because he held the woman to a higher standard of conversation, this question quickly becomes a personal attack regarding his love and who it is "supposedly" geared toward the most. Therefore, his choosing not to answer is because he's chalking it up (in his mind) as a misstatement on her part that he refuses to entertain, which may turn into a full-blown argument. Women, beware, there are men who make no qualms about being a "mama's boy", but if the man you're with isn't that type, don't stir the pot – leave well enough alone.

1 Corinthians 13:11 (NLT): *When I was a child, I spoke and thought and reasoned as a child. But when I grew up, I put away childish things.*

18. What is your credit score?

The phase of the relationship a woman asks this question in determines whether he should or shouldn't and will or won't answer. Normally it's in the pre-dating "getting to know one another" phase when a man should not or will not answer this question. Why? Because it would be considered too soon to ask such a personal question. Asking at this stage could easily conjure doubts [i.e., moving too fast, ulterior motives, etc.] in his mind, resulting in a hindrance of the relationship going forward. Also, asking this question too early could backfire on the woman possibly by tarnishing her reputation with a fallacious label of being "odd". This is definitely a question to be asked when both parties are in a committed relationship.

Ecclesiastes 3:1 (NLT): *For everything there is a season, a time for every activity under heaven.*

19. Do I need to lose some weight?

For some men, they may find it embarrassing and/or feel apprehensive about discussing their (women's) weight. It can be a very sensitive topic due to possibly depicting an unhidden flaw about them. An honest and wise man may not answer just to keep the peace and out of respect for the woman's feelings and self-esteem. Some men feel that if the woman does need to lose weight, she should already know without having to ask him. Therefore, he will not answer to keep from being her reason for blaming and mistreating him. Although she may be aware that she needs to make a health change but stubbornly chooses to believe that she can do it on her own terms, at times he may question her progress as a show of support. Oftentimes, she may not receive it as such and take it more as a judgmental snide remark instead. An idea the man can employ is setting the example with healthy meal choices whenever they're partaking in mealtimes together and continuing praying for her.

Hebrews 12:1 (NLT): *Therefore, since we are surrounded by such a huge crowd of witnesses to the life of faith, let us strip off every weight that slows us down, especially the sin that so easily trips us up. And let us run with endurance the race God has set before us.*

20. Do you dread coming home when I get cranky?

This question alone beckons an argument if answered truthfully, which is why men (in most cases) will elect not to answer. They feel women already know the answer so why foolishly waste time and energy. After all, who would enjoy coming home to someone who is cranky? There's no enjoyment or peace in that. They're also aware that not answering is the lesser of "two evils" because they realize that a passionate discussion [i.e., argument] will ensue whether the question is answered or not and regardless of the answer being "yes" or "no".

Proverbs 21:19 (NIV): *Better to live in a desert than with a quarrelsome and nagging wife.*

Questions From Men That Women Do Not Answer

Questions From Men
That Women Do Not Answer

1. How much money do you make?

A wise woman knows not to ever answer this question, if unmarried. This is a "none of your business" question that men should refrain from asking women they are dating. The intellect of a woman perceives the ulterior motive of a man as him seeking to gather financial information that he can try and get his hands on or have her to support his welfare. However, she knows her purpose in a relationship is not to be his golden goose. Therefore, she does well in guarding her financial information by being ahead of his "game." Is she wrong? Certainly, NOT!

Matthew 7:6 (NLT): *"Don't waste what is holy on people who are unholy. Don't throw your pearls to pigs! They will trample the pearls, then turn and attack you.*

2. Where do you want to go eat? What do you want for dinner?

Many women will answer either of these questions without hesitation; however, there are those who simply will not answer. The differing factor is partly based on cultural environment [i.e., urban verses rural, ethnical beliefs/practices, etc.]. For those who do not answer, it's not so much that they're unsure of what they'd like to eat. Some are polite by respectfully yielding to their mate to decide, some prefer the mate to surprise them, and some simply don't care because they'll find something they like wherever the mate decides. A woman not providing an answer is no reason for a man to get bent out of shape, just exercise love and patience – no answer is her answer for him to decide.

Proverbs 31:26 (NLT): *When she speaks, her words are wise, and she gives instructions with kindness.*
Ephesians 5:33 (NLT): *So again I say, each man must love his wife as he loves himself, and the wife must respect her husband.*

3. Are you paying for dinner?

If this question is being asked in a platonic relationship, it may be fitting to warrant an answer. However, if dating or married, there are women who will be insulted by her partner asking such a thing; the reason being it is based on cultural environment [i.e., urban verses rural, ethnic beliefs/practices, religion, etc.]. A common viewpoint is that it is considered disrespectful and unbecoming of a gentlemen to ask a lady this question. She sees it as him demeaning his value of her as well as reneging on his "responsibility" as a man taking care of her. Is it a great argument? Well, if it matters to her, it should matter to him – adjust for a happier life.

Ephesians 5:28 (TMB): *Husbands, go all out in your love for your wives, exactly as Christ did for the church—a love marked by giving, not getting.*

4. Did you pass gas?

Yes, you've read it correctly. This is a question a few men wanted investigated as to why some women will not provide a response. The answer is simple: it's embarrassing, and they prefer to just let it pass over (literally). For a woman to be called out on hygiene in any form is considered contemptuous in her opinion. If a woman's hygiene is to be called into question, men should exercise caution and politeness and avoid making light of it. When it comes to hygienic matters, some women can handle the forwardness and others are very sensitive and recoil from discussing them.

1 John 1:8 (TLB): *If we say that we have no sin, we are only fooling ourselves and refusing to accept the truth.*

5. How much do you weigh?

If a man ever wants to get on a woman's bad side, all he must do is question her weight. Why is weight such an emotional topic for many women? They understand that men are visually driven by what they see in a woman, therefore they're highly sensitive about their looks. Many women take it as a personal attack to have their weight questioned (especially in a negative or sarcastic manner) by their partner – and, NO, it doesn't matter if the man is just asking in general or is asking to compliment her on how well she may be taking care herself. This is proven based on their defensive verbal response along the lines of "Look at you, as though you're all that!" or abruptly cutting the conversation short with a perturbed facial expression. Men must be mindful about how conditions [i.e., having children, taking care of children, menstrual cycles, stress, eating disorders, etc.] affect the body of a woman. Some conditions may be natural and out of her hands, whereas others may be induced. Regardless, men must exercise wisdom, graciousness, and creative motivation without casting judgment and/or coming across as sarcastic.

Romans 7:15 (TLB): *I don't understand myself at all, for I really want to do what is right, but I can't. I do what I don't want to—what I hate.*

6. How old are you?

This question is often a double standard; whereas it is okay for women to ask men their ages, it is not okay for men to ask women. Although there are varying reasons some women take exception to being questioned about their age, one of the most palpable is their taking it as a personal attack because of equating age with their attractiveness. Unfortunately, some women place so much confidence in their looks and are deeply and emotionally wounded when men introduce age. For many of these women, it's a psychological idea that a woman must maintain an appearance of her actual age or less than. To be questioned about their age brings about an automatic, baseless thought that the man views her as being unattractively older. To eliminate any further discussion or the guy guessing an age upward of her true age, she just chooses not to answer. On the other hand, there are men who ask just to be careful of not getting involved with someone significantly younger that could cause legal issues for them – better to be safe by asking the women than by criminally answering the law.

Proverb 31:30 (TLB): *Charm can be deceptive and beauty doesn't last, but a woman who fears and reverences God shall be greatly praised.*

7. How many intimate partners have you had?

A wise woman knows when and what to speak protect her character. Many women assume or know that answering this question truthfully can and/or will have dire consequences that will dash any hopes of a relationship leading to marriage with their present partner. So, what do they do? Either minimize the count or not answer at all. Not answering at all may be the most intelligent move due to understanding that the 'past is the past' and what is being established with the present partner should be the focus for building a future. There are emotions of regret, shame, and hurt that come with keeping count of past intimate partners; therefore, such a question warrants no response.

Proverbs 29:20 (NIV): *Do you see someone who speaks in haste? There is more hope for a fool than for them.*

8. Are you promiscuous?

For some women to not answer this question means the answer is "yes." Those are women who are not ready for a committed relationship, enjoy playing the field and are comfortable having no convictions about their way of life. They dare any man to impede on what they find satisfying by asking such a question, which they consider offensive. Then there are those women who do not answer because of being appalled by the question. They take it as either the man sees them as easy prey or is alluding to what type of relationship he's looking for; hence, they refuse to waste a second of time entertaining what they consider to be an absurd question.

Proverbs 31:3 (TMB): *Don't dilute your strength on fortune-hunting women, promiscuous women who shipwreck leaders.*

9. Can you handle your insecurities and my vulnerability?

Not answering about handling her insecurities signifies she either believes she has none or is insulted by the man implying she does. Not answering about his vulnerability implies an expectation of hers that he should not be vulnerable or the false notion that "real" men do not have vulnerabilities – those who do she may consider to be less than men. Notwithstanding, her refusal to answer can result in the formation of emotional barriers with her mate in the long-term. The enemy loves to operate within these barriers that isolate both partners. He uses what couples withhold from one another as a tool to stir either both or one partner in going outside the relationship, and seeking another to "understand and help" with whatever the insecurity or vulnerability issues may be – all to the destruction of a covenanted union that could have been avoided by them communicating with one another. Truth be known, it is healthy to recognize, appreciate, and properly manage insecurities and/or vulnerabilities – they help us remain modest when we get off track by focusing on them in the lives of others. It's in our uncertainties and weaknesses that we can be made strong by the love and support of our partners and vice versa.

Mark 10:9 (NIV): *Therefore, what God has joined together, let no one separate.*
2 Corinthians 12:10 (NLT): *Two people are better off than one, for they can help each other succeed.*

10. Is marriage a business transaction?

This question can be taken cynically, resulting in her snubbing the idea of the man having the audacity to ask such a question. For most women, marriage is taken seriously and for a lifetime. From their perspective, the image of seeing marriage as a business transaction would be an insult to the high regard of the custom that "seals the deal" between two people for life. Furthermore, having a man present

132

this question may put a sour taste in her mouth about going forward with the relationship. Is it a bad question to ask? No. However, it must be asked in a respectful manner for the sake of him making sure they're both on the same page.

Proverbs 15:27 (NLT): *Greed brings grief to the whole family, but those who hate bribes will live.*

11. Are you seeing, still in contact with old friends?

Right off the bat, she's probably assuming he's speaking of male friends. In such instances, guilty parties will not answer for one of two reasons: reason one may be because she's trying to see the best in the man but he's now showing a sign of poor self-control, instability, obsession, and/or someone seeking to micromanage who she can or cannot connect with as old friends. Reason two may be because her old friends are still considered her friends and they are who she turns to in times of need. Either way, a mature woman can hold her own by being honest and a mature man would understand. If further discussion is needed, it can be done cordially and respectfully. However, if those old/new friends are heavily influencing the woman's every decision to the point where it is truly interfering with the relationship between she and her mate, something has to give. Priority of friendship begins with having God as a friend and allowing that relationship to pour into the relationship between husband and wife.

Mark 10:9 (NIV): *Therefore, what God has joined together, let no one separate.*

12. What did you and your ex do sexually?

A definite no-no! This question deserves no answer and is quite weird and inappropriate for any mate to ask. For those who don't know why, those encounters were private and offer no value whatsoever to the current relationship. Asking this question is a show of disrespect to the current relationship as well as to the intelligence of the woman. A man that is wanting to know the answer to this question is not a man who should be taken serious as a partner. As a matter of fact, he would be a man any woman should stay clear of. For those women who see fit to answer this question (for whatever reason), his companionship will soon be to your sorrow.

Proverbs 12:23 (NLT): *The wise don't make a show of their knowledge but fools broadcast their foolishness.*

13. What did...(someone else's private matter)?

She doesn't answer anything pertaining to someone else's business because she is a woman of character, integrity, and virtue. That means more to her than being in a relationship with a nosey partner. She's a friend indeed and will not compromise nor sacrifice that no matter who or what it may cost her. A man asking this question is displaying immature feminine tendencies. How does someone else's personal business affect his? If it does, it would be best for him to confront the person(s) as a mature adult to iron things out, instead of risking putting his partner in an uncomfortable compromising position that may cost the relationship. The woman who doesn't blabbermouth the personal affairs of others is a woman who can truly be trusted and considered as a confidant.

Proverbs 11:13 (NLT): *A gossip goes around telling secrets, but those who are trustworthy can keep a confidence.*

14. Have you had an abortion?

This is a very sensitive topic and private matter which is inappropriate for a man to ask, if he and she do not have a trust-bonded relationship. A few possible reasons a woman chooses not to answer could be her not owing anyone an explanation, embarrassment, regret, trust issues, etc. Her making the decision to have an abortion was not made lightly and may have taken a toll on her mentally, emotionally, and physically; therefore, it is not up for a shoot-the-breeze discussion. However, if this question is asked by a partner who she's in a serious relationship with (possibly leading to marriage), engaged or married to, it is worth having this discussion maturely. The air needs to be cleared regarding both their feelings about current children (either may have), plans for having children, and/or stances on abortion.

Romans 3:23-24 (NLT): *For everyone has sinned; we all fall short of God's glorious standard. Yet God, in his grace, freely makes us right in his sight. He did this through Christ Jesus when he freed us from the penalty for our sins.*

15. Have you cheated on your spouse before?

Here are three common reasons a woman may not answer this question: she's seeking to move beyond the past because of the shame; still prone to cheating; or offended by the question. The first two reasons are more understandable than the third so let's address why. Many women appreciate, respect, and find security in the admiration their mates have for and exhibit toward them. That fondness can be disrupted for some women who would consider it a tremendous insult for a man to imply such a specious insinuation of her ever cheating in a relationship. Although the man is not saying she has cheated and is only asking a need-to-know question for his awareness, she takes it as a betrayal of trust and a personal attack against her character. Although it isn't an off-the-table question, it is one that a man must be careful about asking and sensitive in how it is presented.

Matthew 15:19 (TLB): *For from the heart come evil thoughts, murder, adultery, fornication, theft, lying, and slander.*

16. What's your bra size?

This is a question that should only be asked of a WIFE when a HUSBAND is planning to purchase gift lingerie for her. Otherwise, this question is very inappropriate and invasive. With men being visual, it's very easy for them to discreetly take notice and distinguish whether a woman's bosom size satisfies his preference without having to ask for specifics. More than likely a woman declining to answer is because it's insulting and embarrassing, which may lead to her seeing the man as creepy and disrespectful – only wanting her because of what he sees rather than who she is entirely. It is beneficial for men to learn and behave like gentlemen rather than being adult males with a juvenile imprudent mentality.

Ephesians 4:14 (TLB): *Then we will no longer be like children, forever changing our minds about what we believe because someone has told us something different or has cleverly lied to us and made the lie sound like the truth.*

17. What's your credit score?

This is a tough one due to not knowing the reason behind a man asking. Is he asking to determine whether he can use her credit to support his material wants and needs? Or is he asking to ensure she is well within a good score range as he is (to alleviate linking with a woman who will soon be a financial burden)? Women do not answer this question more than likely because of either bad experiences with guys in the past, believing false statements about ALL men being up to no good, embarrassment by actually having a below average credit score, or just being extremely careful. Either reason is her choice, but if she's in a relationship with someone and marriage seems promising (from both of their perspectives), it would be advantageous for them to have a heart-to-heart financial discussion (credit score inclusive).

Proverbs 24:27 (NLT): *Do your planning and prepare your fields before building your house.*

18. Have you been arrested before?

Not answering is a strong implication of "YES!" Believe it or not (facetiously speaking), there are women with criminal records. There's some embarrassment in almost everyone's past and by human nature it is not something to be proud of nor easy to share. The risk of sharing can cost what was perceived as a promising relationship, shattering all hopes and dreams of escaping a record of error. That is why some women do not answer. Others may not answer because of being insulted by the question. After all, they have it "all together" and they dare any man to see anything criminal about them. Yet, they feel it's okay for them to ask a guy this question. Nonetheless, this question is worth discussing prior to marriage and pride should never come before truth. God can change hearts and work all things for the good.

Romans 12:2 (ESV): *Do not be conformed to this world, but be transformed by the renewal of your mind, that by testing you may discern what is the will of God, what is good and acceptable and perfect.*

19. Have you ever or are you currently seeing a therapist?

Many men would consider it disturbing for a woman not to answer this question, as important as it is. It could erroneously leave them [i.e., men] with a false assumption that the answer is not only "yes" but is evident by the woman's behavior – leading to a possible loss of what could've been a great relationship. Women who do not answer are simply overly cautious and/or imposing an act of need-to-know privacy only. They may feel ashamed or very protective of disclosing this type of personal information – let alone the risk of costing them a bright relationship with "Mr. Right." However, if in a serious relationship (especially engaged or married), it is imperative for this question to be answered and discussed in detail with her partner and vice versa. Engaged and/or married couples must operate beyond selfish approaches and be willing to support one another for and through good and bad.

Proverbs 12:15 (LB): *A fool thinks he needs no advice, but a wise man listens to others.*

20. Have you considered suicide?

A sensitive question and topic that requires an answer and/or further discussion. To not answer is ironically answering "yes." Although reasons vary for a woman not to answer, prominent reasons may be humiliation, apprehension about being judged, or maybe still dealing with an issue that triggers the thought of suicide. Being in a relationship calls for honesty and loyalty to one another. If it is the early stages of a relationship, there's nothing wrong with not answering; however, if and when the relationship becomes serious, it's definitely time to discuss suicide matters. Keeping it to self only robs the woman of a full and thriving life with a caring husband. During discussion, it is not a time for a man to show machismo. He must be wise, sensitive, and supportive in every way possible – most importantly he must listen and respond with an understanding compassion.

John 10:10 (NLV): *The robber comes only to steal and to kill and to destroy. I came so they might have life, a great full life.*

21. Have you had any cosmetic surgeries?

For some women who have had cosmetic surgery they will definitely not appreciate this question. Their logic is that the more natural they appear, it should go without questioning. The moment cosmetic surgery is brought into the conversation about them it simply destroys their confidence and esteem because doubt about themselves and/or the cosmetic surgery is introduced. Unless married and it is known for certain that she has had cosmetic surgery, men may want to keep this question off the table if his plans are to remain in a promising relationship with her.

1 Peter 3:3-4 (NLT): *Don't be concerned about the outward beauty of fancy hairstyles, expensive jewelry, or beautiful clothes. You should clothe yourselves instead with the beauty that comes from within, the unfading beauty.*
Proverbs 31:30 (NLV): *Pleasing ways lie and beauty comes to nothing, but a woman who fears the LORD will be praised.*

21. Have you had any cosmetic surgery?

In Closing

The hope is that *It's in Their D.N.A.: What and Why Men and Women Do Not Ask and Do Not Answer* will prove to be a valuable resource for closing respective conversation gaps in male and female relationships. Although there is no one self-help relationship book that has all the answers, each brings something beneficial to the table. The purpose of this book is to help ask, answer, and decipher questions that matter for building healthy and everlasting relationships. While there is nothing unique about what is written in this book, it provides central source for gathering useful questions that can and should be injected in serious relationship conversations as well as for understanding what and why certain questions are not answered by the sexes. Lastly, allow your relationship with God to be a prototype of what you're seeking with your mate – be blessed!

Note

Biblical scriptures and various versions (AMP, ESV, MEV, MSG, NCV, NIV, NLT, NLV, TLB, and TMB). BibleGateway. Retrieved from https://www.biblegateway.com/passage/

Author Owen Watson, Ph.D.

Read biography and get an exclusive inside look at exciting upcoming new titles

www.drowenwatson.com

Email: drowenwatson@outlook.com

BOOKS BY
Author Owen Watson, Ph.D.

Relentless Grace: Behind the Scenes of Men

There is Jesus: Prayers for Life's Journey

Prayers for Life's Journey

Fighting Cancer One Poem a Day
(50 states & D.C. series)

Behind My Glorious Smile
(by Antoinette Thomas & Owen Watson, Ph.D.)

Betting on Me: Revelatory Concepts for Success

Defeating Cancer One Poem a Day

Po' Man Ain't Got Not Much Say

What Matters Most: Family, Friends, and Foes

www.ingramcontent.com/pod-product-compliance
Lightning Source LLC
Chambersburg PA
CBHW060248050426

42448CB00009B/1597